WHAT OTHERS ARE SAYING...

Out of Havana provides an uncommon ordinary woman's insight into the last half century of Cuba's tumultuous recent history. More powerfully than an academic study or historical account, it allows us intimately to grasp the enthusiasm, commitment and sense of promise that defined many average Cubans' experience of the 1959 Revolution and the first triumphant decades of the Castro regime. As the story shifts into the final decades of the last century (the 1980s Mariel Boatlift, the so-called "special period in time of peace" [from 1991 to the end of the decade], and the 1994 Balseros or Rafters Crisis), it starts gradually to reveal, with understated yet relentless eloquence, an ultimately insuperable rift between the high-flown official rhetoric of uncompromising struggle and revolutionary sacrifice and the harsh conditions and cruelly absurd situations that the protagonist, along with the majority of Cubans, begin routinely to live out. It is a rare and important document, a unique personal chronicle of an everyday Cuban reality that most Americans continue to know only fragmentarily.

— *Luís Madureira, Co-Editor of the Luso-Brazilian Review, Professor and Chair of the Department of Spanish and Portuguese, University of Wisconsin-Madison, USA*

Born in Havana in 1969 to two high-ranking officers with the MININT and now living in Spain, I found every page laden with powerful and evocative experiences that reawakened so many memories. Fascinating, accurate and engaging but without sentimentality, the book succeeds in capturing an intense period in history that anyone wanting to understand today's Cuba should read. A vivid portrait of how revolution can become a synonym of regression, and truth is entirely relative.

— *Dr. Slava López Rodríguez, Strategic Project Manager at the University of Granada, Education Research Methods instructor at the University of Seville, Spain.*

Anyone concerned to understand the dynamics and the meaning of the Cuban Revolution needs to move beyond the confines of a structural analysis, for which there are numerous published sources, into the subjective experience of people who have 'lived' the revolutionary process over time. This book does so via the imagined voices of ordinary Cuban women based on anthropological research and a 'creative non-fictional account of these voices. Not everyone will agree with the author's imaginative reconstruction an discursive account of the revolutionary process as experienced from within. But a must read for anyone interested in understanding the full meaning of the Revolution.

—*Henry Veltmeyer, Professor of Development,
Universidad Autónoma de Zacatecas, Mexico*

A fascinating narrative allowing us to bear witness to the complexities and contradictions of state revolutionary consciousness in terms of women's lives.

—*Jamie Magnusson, Adult Education and Community Development,
OISE, University of Toronto, Canada*

"Out of Havana" will be thought provoking for anyone fascinated by the complexities of social change. By creatively synthesizing her academic research into one woman's story, Dr. Alonso powerfully shares what she learned about the promises, joys, contradictions, disappointments, and failures of the Cuban Revolution.

—*Nancy Worcester, Professor Emerita, Department of Gender &
Women's Studies, University of Wisconsin-Madison, USA*

Araceli Alonso

OUT OF HAVANA

MEMOIRS OF ORDINARY LIFE IN CUBA

Deep University Press
Blue Mounds, Wisconsin

Deep University Online !

For updates and more resources
Visit the Deep University Website:
www.deepuniversity.com

Copyright © 2014 by Poiesis Creations Ltd - *Deep University Press*
Member of Independent Book Publishers Association (IBPA)

All rights reserved. No part of this book may be reproduced in any form, by Photostat, microfilm, retrieval system, or any other means, without prior written permission of the publisher.
For permissions, contact: publisher@deepuniversity.net

ISBN 9781-939755-03-2 (pb)
Library of Congress Cataloging-in-Publication Data
1. Hispanic Culture. 2. Cuba. 3. Narrative Inquiry. 4. Women Studies.
3. Multicultural Studies. 4. Alonso, Araceli

Keywords: Araceli Alonso, Latin American Studies, Creative Non-Fiction, Women's Ethnography, Women's Lives, Personal Narrative, Life History, Cuba, Havana, Cuban Women, Cuban Revolution, Caribbean Studies, Marxism, Socialism, Memoir.

Target audience: Undergraduate Students, Graduate Students, College Instructors, General Public.

Version 3
Proofreading: Saylín Alvárez, James Bucklew, Biruté Ciplijauskaité
Cover: Marcos Colón (design) & François V. Tochon (text selection)
Cover captions by Marcos Colón (front) and Liliane Calfee (back)

CONTENTS

What Others are Saying	1
Contents	5
Acknowledgments	6
Note of the Author	8
Foreword by Madeline Camara	9
Introduction	11
Out of Havana	17
Chapter 1 Life at the solar	22
Chapter 2 Santa Bárbara and Ochún	33
Chapter 3 Nothing went back to normal	46
Chapter 4 Donde digo 'digo' digo 'Diego'	64
Chapter 5 Love and Revolution	71
Chapter 6 Good-Bye!	86
Chapter 7 Moscú Rojo and other red products	97
Chapter 8 The sea inside	104
Chapter 9 Reading Orwell in Havana	112
Chapter 10 Ave, Fidel! Cubans Morituri te salutant	128
Chapter 11 Es-Cuba diving	142
Chapter 12 Happily Ever Before	155
Chapter 13 Cuba NoVa	176
Chapter 14 When God came to Havana	190
Epilogue	202
Glossary	205
About the Author	220

*To the Cuban Revolution,
for challenging my way of thinking*

Acknowledgments

Although this book would not have been possible without the assistance of many people from both sides of the strait of Florida, my first thanks go to Rosa María Tejedor and to all the women in Cuba who shared their memories and their lives with me. They were the ones who designed my work showing me through their stories paths I could never have imagined. They made me believe I was doing something important in keeping their stories alive. I will be forever indebted to them, and I am aware that my words cannot fully express the importance for me of having met them.

For their early guidance, I am also indebted to University of Wisconsin-Madison professors Maria Lepowsky, Frank Salomon, Kirin Narayan, Nancy Worcester, Mariamne Whatley, Franco Scarano, Betty Hasselkus and Biruté Ciplijauskaité; their enthusiasm with my work made me believe I could write something special.

To the other side of the Strait of Florida, the southern side, my big thanks go to Luisa Campuzano, Dixie Edith Trinquete, Dalia Acosta, Perla Popowsky, Violeta Waterland Díaz, Teresa Orosa, Patricia Arés, Norma Vasallo, Rosa Maria Rovira, and Jorge Yglesias. Their advice, support, cooperation and interest in my work were invaluable and made my research possible.

My friends Saylín Álvarez, James Bucklew, Arsenio Cicero, Diane Soles, and Debbie Greenland deserve a very especial acknowledgment since they gifted me with their very valuable comments and edits through the entire process of my writing. My immense gratitude go to James who meticulously edited the manuscript, and to Saylín and Luís who walked with me through every step of this path believing I could pull these stories together.

For her caring support, I would like to thank my daughter Sofía who enjoyed and suffered every moment of her mother's fieldwork in Havana. And finally, from the deepest part of my heart, a big thank to my husband Antonio for his all-enabling love. From the very first day, Antonio took a *jabita* in his pocket and walked Havana up and down looking for food to feed us. For his long hours of waiting in the lines and because he was the one who made me think I could survive my fieldwork when I was almost determined to give it up.

Note of the Author

I thought of beginning this book with a disclaimer, but that would call into question the truth of this story. The events related actually happened, although the people in the story may whish that they hadn't. While perhaps even neighbors, friends, and family will not be able to recognize the principal protagonists, every "ordinary" family in Cuba will identify with the stories told. Since art and truth are not mutually exclusive, the people in the story and the author have created this book through the arts of telling, listening, and writing.

Foreword

Dr. Madeline Camara
Professor of Latin American Literature
University of South Florida

Watching it rain in Havana ... but instead from the balcony of my house in Weeki Wachee. The story transported me back to the dampness of my city after those sudden downpours so intense and seemingly never ending. I couldn't stop reading it despite an aversion to the electronic screen. The style of this edition captured me, the subtle humorous subtitles, even the font style. Structure and format are united to deliver the transmitted message. They are like the book itself, warm, direct and communicative. Out Of Havana obligates one to be ready to hear a story, no matter how anonymous or how much of it be truth or fiction. Art and truth can not be in conflict the author warns us. She, with a magic stolen form the Yorubas, weaves an oral discourse, evoking the precise words for memories to flow and with them deliver her fragmented story. What appears is a human life, any life, but one that is sufficient to tell the story of a nation and much more besides.

At the beginning of the 21 century, feminism has rescued Marxist thought, bringing theoretical credibility to materialistic approximations to literature and art, so-called Cultural Studies, or New Anthropology. Araceli Alonso knows this, she studies it and has obtained academic degrees in this field. Armed with this knowledge, she travels the world healing other women. She also did her part in Cuba. Story telling was therapy for "Rosa". It has also been for me on this rainy night in northern Florida.

Thank you for reminding me of what is essential, historical facts can not be neglected, yet this story can only be told from some place deep inside. Thus to the reader arrives a story, novelized of a nation torn apart by its own fantasies characteristic of an island and brought about by the isolation of a dictator and a system.

Constructed partly of fiction, testament, anthropology and intelligent observation, this empathetic story doesn't leave out anything of the actual history nor of any literary recourses at the disposition of an author disposed to tell it. A country where its roots are intertwined, where there exist at least two economic systems, the official and the informal, where the dissidence defies the power structure both in private and in public; a narcissistic nation which has always loved show more than truth, needful of many voices and bodies in order to leave archived this chronicle of love and rage that has been the Cuban Revolution.

Introduction

Dr. Araceli Alonso
University of Wisconsin—Madison

This book is the product of a long gestation, many hours of recording, many others of listening and much reflection and research over the structural changes brought about by the Cuban Revolution and its deep impact on real people's lives. The stories in this book were told to me in pieces, disconnected and fragmented, not making much sense at first. It was in the process of telling that the stories made sense for the people who told them, and it was in the process of writing, selecting, compiling, and framing that they did for me.

Using the lens of life-story to identify and examine contradictions between public discourse and lived experience in women's lives, this book reviews the history of Cuba of the last twentieth century, especially the Revolution of 1959 and its aftermath, reconstructing Cuban historical experience as lived by four generations of Cuban women within the same family. Rosa[1], the main narrative voice in the story, belonged to the cohort of women who were born during the years of Fulgencio Batista's repressive and violent dictatorship. Their adolescence was filled with the dreams and enthusiasm of the 1959 Revolution. They matured, and to different degrees were committed to the strict communism of the early revolutionary years. As they grew older,

---

[1] Individuals in this book selected new identities for themselves, choosing names that according to them "matched their personalities."

however, they embarked in yet another Cuba, one in which charity, delirium, disorder, and disillusion became the fabric of their daily lives.

Throughout this book, I have used the parallel between the revolutionary process and the personal life-cycle to examine women's experiences within the framework of the Cuban reality. This metaphor illuminates the way in which the Cuban Revolution, itself a metaphor, has profoundly marked women's passage through periods of adjustment and growth. Rendering Rosa's narrative in this format allowed me to follow the developmental stages of her adult life, juxtaposing her voice with the historical and cultural progress of the Cuban Revolution. In this way, her story highlights the complexities, the ambiguities, and the contradictions that Cuban women have contended with, and continue to contend with, in both their social and private lives. The picture that emerges challenges the official Cuban discourse on women's lives under the Revolution, offering an alternative to existing stereotypes and assumptions.

Rosa's life was filled with contrasts within which she often seemed to have moved without much difficulty. She lived her infancy surrounded by black *Ochún* and Catholic *La Caridad del Cobre* without finding any contradiction between the two at all. In 1959, Rosa joined the new Revolution with enthusiasm and idealism. She undertook her participation as both a personal battle for her own rights and as a duty to Cuban society. She joined the labor force, did volunteer work, and took the slogans of the Socialist Revolution as her own. As a *compañera* (comrade), Rosa forgot her Catholic prayers and hid her saints, and she also erased the memory of her loved ones in exile. She cut sugar cane, harvested coffee, taught reading and writing, and repudiated imperialism and the U.S. dollar as expressions of the enemy's degradation of humans. As a young woman, Rosa went out from her home to become *miliciana* (member of the National Revolutionary Militia), defender of a Revolution that would show the rest of the world that Cuba was strong and that socialism was the answer to the world's problems. Those were the years when Rosa would exchange the *Orishas* (Yoruba deities and spirits) and the Gospels for the Russian dictionary and named one of her children Boris, as the new Soviet fashion dictated. Rosa also assimilated a new way of talking, a military language and a military way of life. She talked about *el núcleo del partido* (communist party cell), *el suministro del batallón* (army provisions), *el comité organizador* (organizing committee), and *la comisión política* (political commission). Rosa, however, did not only learn military terminology but also actively prepared to defend her homeland and attack the enemy in the great battle that was always imminent—but never came.

By 1980, after twenty years of Socialist Revolution, Rosa had made substantial gains under Fidel Castro's regime. She no longer had to face giving birth without medical attention or fear that she would not be able to provide her children with the minimum necessities of food, clothing, and basic medical and dental care. Furthermore, access to contraception and abortion, the elimination of domestic servitude and prostitution, universal education, and state policies that encouraged women's employment brought Rosa's generation of women greater economic independence and more diverse professional opportunities than ever before. In the late 1980's, however,—she did not remember exactly when—after almost thirty years of Cuban socialism, Rosa began to question her life. She noted her lack of freedom to control her own personal life. She saw that she had very little authority in the construction of her own life or her children's. In fact, she participated very little in drafting the policies that governed the country. Her gains, she began to think, were achieved at a very high price. She felt tremendously lonely and worn out. She saw that her children had grown up closer to the state than to her and her husband; they were distant strangers even while living in the same home. She also saw how her closest relatives and friends had seemed ready to leave at a moment's notice for *p'allá enfrente* ("over there;" Miami); she lost her sister and father through emigration. Family, crucial for Rosa, broke into two halves, split between Cuba and its northern counterpart, Miami. Deep feelings of loneliness, guilt, remorse, and disillusionment began to be part of her daily life.

In the 1990s, the once young *compañera* was in her fifties. With the end of her reproductive cycle came the Russian Perestroika, and then later the Cuban *Periodo Especial en Tiempos de Paz* (Special Period in Times of Peace*).* As occurred in the early years of the Revolution, Rosa was required again to shed her identity to meet the new needs of the nation. In the past, right after the Revolution, she was called to become a "heroine of work" and prodded to do better than her mother and grandmother through joining the labor force. Ironically during the 1990s, Rosa would be call to become the "heroine of home," thus losing her identity as a working woman and returning to the roles of her own grandmother in the early years of the 20th Century. The collapse of state socialism in Eastern Europe and in the Soviet Union, and the new mandates of the Cuban Revolution with its "survival at all costs" changed the way many Cuban women, including Rosa, thought about themselves in relation to their families, to themselves, and to the Revolution at the same time that other problems such as prostitution, delinquency, and racism reemerged on the island.

For Rosa, to remain loyal to state socialism was the only answer in time of crisis; any other alternative would threaten the nation. However, experiencing deep cuts in living standards, Rosa defied the law and the official exhortations. When the value of her official salary plunged, she turned to prohibited private enterprises and participated in the black market both as buyer and a seller. Without directly attacking socialism, Rosa withdrew her support for the Revolution; she also returned to religion. She refused the call to do more volunteer work when subsistence became more time-consuming for her, and instead used her time in illegal private economic activity. Rosa did not call either for an end of socialism or for a capitalist revolution; she just tried to make the best of a bad situation.

After more than thirty years of being what she called a "deep revolutionary," Rosa began invoking her spirits again, rescued the statues of her forgotten saints and brought back to life the memories of those who left *p'al norte* (to the North, Miami). Her military language, in absence of a real enemy, became part of her domestic battle: *déjame ver si traigo una brigada para que me pinte la cocina* (let me see if I can get a brigade to come and paint my kitchen); *nosotras deberíamos atrincherarnos en la bodega porque muchacha, tanto chícharo y tanto pan de boniato ya no hay quien lo resista* (we should go set up camp in the supply store because, girl, we're all sick of so much yellow beans and sweet potato bread); and *aquí me tienes, en la lucha* (here I am, fighting in the battle). With her militia language, Rosa incorporated in times of the *Periodo Especial* new terms that she shared with her daughter and granddaughter such as *no es fácil; estoy complicada; déjame ver que invento para comer; hoy no resolví; la calle está mala; la guagua está imposible; ya ves, le salió el bombo y se fue p'al Yuma* (it's difficult; I have trouble; let me see what I can invent today to eat; today I couldn't scrape things together; there's nothing to buy in the streets; the buses never come; they won the emigration lottery and went to the United States).

From the Catholicism of her childhood Rosa preserved a crucifix, a cracked figurine of Saint Lazarus made of clay, and a little portrait of St. Barbara. From the capitalism of her youth, Rosa inherited the notion that material incentive is somehow necessary for the functioning of society. From socialism Rosa acquired the understanding that when there is nothing to share, all people receive the same nothing. From the Revolution Rosa took dozens of diplomas and decorations: the outstanding worker, the most dedicated worker, and the worker of the year. As for "Castroism," Rosa came to the opinion that "Fidel tried hard to get to Utopia, but he got lost in the attempt."

It's night and Havana is quiet. It's as if Rosa's death woke up a part of my memory, or perhaps I had been too lazy to remember thinking that Rosa would keep her story forever.

The day I learned of Rosa's death, Isabelita had sent me an e-mail that left me paralyzed and disconcerted, "My mom died, she drowned in a plate of soup. I thought you'd like to know. I tried to write to you yesterday but the electricity was gone."

I rushed to call Rosa's neighbor to find out what had really happened, but I realized I didn't have an international phone service that allowed calls to Cuba from the United States. I hurried to Walgreens to buy a calling card that would allow me to call Havana for a very few minutes at a much higher rate than calling Tokyo or Kuala Lumpur. I dialed the eleven-digit calling-card number, the ten-digit pin code, the three-digit international code, the two-digit country code, the one-digit city code, and the six-digit phone number to Rosa's neighbors.

"*¡Oigo!*"[1] I hear!

"Elvira? This is Ara speaking."

"*¡Oigo! ¡Oigo! ¡Se cayó la llamada!*"[2]

"No, no, I am still here, Elvira, it's me Ara. I can hear you, don't hang up!"

The telephone clicked and Elvira's voice vanished. I dialed the thirty-three numbers again.

"*¡Oigo!*"

---

1. I'm listening.
2. The connection cut off.

"Elvira, this is Ara."

"*No, mi amor.*[3] This is Angelina. Hang up and dial again for Elvirita."

Crap! I'd forgotten that Elvira, via an intricate maze of wires, had rigged up an extension enabling her two next-door neighbors to share her phone for the charge of twenty *pesos* a month. The three households connected by this complex extension system shared the same telephone number, and it wasn't unusual that one of the neighbors without knowing that somebody else in another house was on the phone, tried to make an outgoing call.

"Hey, hang up! I'm speaking!"

Although anyone could answer the phone, it seemed that everybody knew for whom the phone was ringing, "Don't pick up the phone, it's for Jorge's son," Elvira often said.

"Elvira, is that you?"

"¡*Sí, oigo!*"

"This is Ara, I am calling from *El Norte*. Isabelita wrote me saying that her mother passed away."

"Oh, yes, poor Rosi, she wasn't feeling well."

"How did it happen?"

"She was eating a *puré San Germán* with Kati and Camila and suddenly fell over her plate, face down, and drowned."

"This only happens in Cuba," I thought.

The phone beeped and a recorded voice announced that the time was nearly up.

"Please Elvira, tell Isabelita that I'll be in Havana as soon as I can."

---

3. No, honey.

No matter that I held a European passport, I would have to travel illegally to the forbidden island. The ordinance of the U.S. Department of State couldn't be more explicit: "Any person subject to U.S. jurisdiction who engages in any travel-related transaction in Cuba violates the U.S. Department of Treasury regulations. Failure to comply may result in civil penalties and criminal prosecution upon return to the United States."

During the past decade, I had traveled to Cuba from all over the world including Spain, Hong Kong, Australia, and Angola, but never from the United States where I lived for more than twenty years; the government restriction even included travel through a third country such as Mexico or Canada. I tried through Canada once, what a disaster!

Chicago-Cancun with American Airlines, and Cancun-Havana with Mexicana de Aviación to avoid suspicion. Fortunately, the Cuban immigration authorities never stamp passports, and the Cuban visa is a simple piece of paper not even stapled in the passport. There would be no evidence that I had traveled to Havana.

It was hard to believe that Rosa was dead. She rested peacefully in her coffin. She didn't look sick, and she had even put on several pounds since I last saw her.

"It's all the sugar and flour that she has eaten in these last few years," Isabelita said, "We even had to order a larger coffin because she didn't fit in the regular one they had at the morgue."

"I don't want my daughter to be buried!" Mima cried insisting she had heard that human skulls had been recently stolen from the Colón cemetery.

"You're right grandma," Pedrito said, "After four decades of Communism there is nothing else left to steal, just skulls."

"Communism has nothing to do with this," Elvira defended angrily. "The *paleros*[4] are the ones who are stealing bones from the graves to do their African sorcery rituals."

"Comooneests arre vood!" shouted Katinka in her particular accent.

"You all shut up! This is not the best time for this shit!" Isa demanded.

"Is Mayda coming?" I asked changing the subject.

"She is trying, but you know how that is. She applied for an emergency visa for her sister's funeral but she had little hope to get it in time," Mima answered.

I don't know whether the communists or the *paleros* are stealing bones from the graves, but indeed the Colón cemetery doesn't look like the one I visited many years ago. The largest and most beautiful cemetery in Latin America has been vandalized. Many of the tombstones and the statues have been removed or broken, and the old beautiful marble pantheons appear more like abandoned shantytowns than eternal resting places. Rosa's casket doesn't fit in the hole that the grave keeper has dug up. I am sweating as three men are trying to lower the casket, forcing it, into the grave.

I keep sweating, the quality of the wood is so bad that I am afraid the coffin is going to crack releasing Rosa's body into the ground. The three men are pushing hard.

"She is too heavy," one of them says.

"She was all skin and bones a few years ago, my poor daughter!" I hear Mima sobbing.

---

4. Practitioners of the *Palo Monte Mayombe* religion, one of the most widespread religions of African descent in Cuba. *Monte* means "forest" and *palo* means "stick." The forest is the *paleros* church and sticks of different plants are key elements in the practice of this Congo religion. *Paleros* are also referred as *mayomberos* or male witches.

"*Compañeros,* do us the favor of finishing fast or we are going to die here under the sun," Angelina complains.

Rosa's casket floats in the air before the three men attempt again to fit it inside the hole. After several tries, the grave keeper gives up. He comes back twenty minutes later with a shovel to make the hole bigger.

Rest in peace, Rosa María, I pray to myself. Now that you are dead, it's up to me to tell your story or bury it with you in this grave. I have chosen the first.

Chapter 1
LIFE AT THE SOLAR

I guess that I had to be born somewhere and sometime, so I did it in Havana, the same year Colonel Fulgencio Batista was elected president of the Republic of Cuba.

"You were born by accident," Mima told me when I was five years old.

Nothing dramatic, really, she got pregnant out of wedlock, and although at that time many couples lived together, had children together, died together, and never put a foot in the Church, for Mima that was a bad accident, and I, Rosa María Tejedor Rodríguez, was the result of such an unforgivable sin. A year and a half later my sister Mayda joined me, another accident for poor Mima.

"I am Catholic, Apostolic, and Roman," Mima said to my father, "and I should have married virgin as God demands. I have two daughters and I'm still *arrimá,* shame on you Ramón!" she protested.

"I'll marry you when I get the money!" Pipo promised her a hundred times.

When Mima got pregnant the third time, she threatened Pipo to take Mayda and me to Matanzas to live with her mother if he didn't marry her soon. That third pregnancy would be the chance for Mima not only to marry Pipo, but also to prove to her mother-in-law that she was not an *hembrera* and could also bear sons, not only daughters. But the baby didn't make it and my father didn't have to fulfill his promise of marrying before the baby was born.

We lived in a tiny dwelling made of wood, surrounded by other dwellings attached to one another by a thin wall. Most dwellings had only one room for everything, basically four walls and a roof. We called that place *solar*. Our house was the last one in the *solar*, and the closest to the *patio*. Across the long and dark hallway there was another line of similar dwellings. There was only one toilet, a latrine really, in the patio for the thirty-something people who lived there; no running water, we took our own buckets and emptied them into it. Sometimes the smell in the hallway by our house was unbearable. There were neighbors, especially children, who couldn't wait to go to the toilet and defecated and urinated outside in the *patio*. They would just shit on the floor and we had to scrape it up and throw it away. Mayda and I had a potty chair that we kept using until we moved out of the *solar*, but it was far from ideal; if the latrine was occupied, we couldn't clean the potty right away and our little house stank like hell.

In the *patio* there was also a sink, and a kind of closet with a shower inside. Our turns for the shower were posted on a piece of cardboard nailed to the wall, with the names of the neighbors. Mayda and I didn't use the shower much, not only because our names had not been written on the list, but also because we preferred to bathe in our house pouring water in with a bucket. When I became a *señorita*, washing my sanitary pads became a torment. Sometimes I stood in the middle of the night to go to the bathroom when most people were sleeping so I could wash my pads in the sink outside and keep them under my bed to dry. I couldn't take the idea of my father and my neighbors seeing those things hanging outside to dry, although my sister and other girls didn't mind. Some well-off girls at the school used *Kotex* instead of cloth pads, and they bragged about their periods showing the box of *Kotex* whenever they had the chance. But Mima used cloth pads and I would have to use them as well; no other option for me.

Mayda and I slept together in a *columbina* that during the day served us as a kind of a high table and as a bed at night. My parents slept in their own bed close to us, only separated by a curtain. Very soon Mayda and I needed to sleep in different beds because I couldn't stop wetting the bed.

"Mima, Mima, Rosi has peed again and I am all soaked," Mayda complained.

I started sleeping in my own *columbina* when I was ten, but in a few months my new mattress was spoiled, full of urine, and I couldn't use it anymore; the mattress would never get totally dry and Mima decided it was time to throw it away when green and black fungus started growing like an army of mushrooms; the smell was horrendous and the heat and humidity of Havana didn't help much. For a while I had to sleep directly over the mattress coils that very soon became rusted and pinched my body. Mima washed and boiled my sheets every day, and to my embarrassment she had to hang them outside in the *patio* to dry.

Some nights I developed a strange and inexplicable frenzy when behind the curtain I heard my parents' voices, their unrest, and their struggle.

"Leave me alone, Ramón. Don't you see I am sleeping?" Mima said when Pipo came back home late after having drunk up his weekly salary.

"Come on, *Vieja*, just a little bit. I am your husband and I have my rights!"

"No, you aren't my husband and you have no rights over me. This is a sin. You can go to hell, but not me."

My father's voice changed and became more authoritative as the bed creaked loudly under the two bodies locked in struggle. Then Mima stopped complaining and I heard the rhythm of a continuous and monotonous movement, shifting gradually from slow now and faster later. Their bed vibrated, my bed vibrated, the whole dwelling vibrated. The curtain between us appeared thinner than ever. I could feel my body and my heart trembling and my breathing growing more rapid. I squeezed my legs until I felt an electric shock all over my body. My frenzy subsided and my respiration grew quiet again. I gradually became calmer breathing with a slow regularity, and I fell asleep, my body bathed in a pool a sweat.

When I was fourteen, Pipo decided to build a room upstairs, that is a *barbacoa*, with the materials he had been storing for months inside our place. When the day came, we covered the furniture with cardboard, and with the help of two neighbors we started the construction. The two neighbors mixed by hand the sand, the gravel, and the Portland cement and put it in a bucket. I was in charge of taking the bucket to the upper level. As Mima filled the bucket I took it up and poured a layer of the concrete over the wooden platform that Pipo had made with the stored planks. Mayda helped, leveling and stomping the concrete. Finally Pipo and the two neighbors put reinforcing bars so Mayda and I wouldn't fall down over my parents' bodies at night. A few days later, Mayda and I could sleep up on the *barbacoa* while my parents had their own place below. Although I couldn't hear my parents as clear as before, once in a while I kept squeezing my legs.

I didn't see Pipo very often. During the day he worked as a janitor at the National Bank of Cuba, and in the evening he worked in a shoe factory, the Goliat-Keds, close to Luyanó, where we lived. His week days were for work, and his weekends for friends and bars. I loved Pipo, anyway. Although as much as I loved him, as much he made me suffer. For years and years, even after I married, I tried to please him, but he always preferred Mayda; she was the apple of his eye, she was Pipo's joy. Mayda would run to hug him while I just waited for him to come to me, which never happened. Mayda would sit on his lap and kiss him while I spied on them with a broken heart. Mayda always knew what she wanted and how to get it from Pipo. Sometimes I heard her saying to him, "Come on, *Viejo*, if you don't buy me the yellow coat I will tell Mima that I saw you with a *fondillúa* last weekend." Smart and shameless Mayda! Pipo laughed hard and bought and did whatever she asked him for.

One of the things I resented the most from Pipo was when during the weekends he took me to the bars where he used to drink and play cards and dominoes with his friends. Pipo would ask me first to wear a nice skirt. I knew what he wanted and I hated it! I went with him. I sat in the bar, watching Pipo's friends play cards and talk obscenities. After a while, when Pipo became a little happy or really drunk, he would say to me: "Now, dance for us, girl!" and he made me dance in front of his drunk friends. How much I hated to dance in front of those jerks! They didn't touch me; it was just this stupid dancing in front of the drooling bastards. The tradition stopped when Mima found out through a neighbor, "If your *papá* asks you to go to the bar with him, tell me first, you understand?" she said to me in a grave tone.

"*¡Viejo sinvergüenza!*" I heard Mima saying, "*¡Descara'o! ¡Maricón!*"

But Pipo was not always as bad. Some weekends, he took us to the cinema where for 20 cents we saw a movie and had a delicious beverage made of strawberries and frappé ice.

Going to the movies and reading were my ways out of the *solar*. At home, I hid behind the big *escaparate* we had on the right corner of our house and I read everything I could get my hands on, like <u>Selecciones</u>, <u>El Diario de la Marina</u>, <u>Vanidades</u>. The *escaparate* was my secret place to dream and cry. Everybody knew I was there, but nobody bothered me, not even Pipo. The novels by Corín Tellado[5] that Mima brought from the houses where she worked as a maid were my favorite. After I read them over and over again, I would go to a second hand bookstore and exchange them for other ones. I could recite some passages by heart, like when María Teresa Cortés overheard her fiancé Alfredo talking to a friend:

---

5. Corín Tellado was a prolific Spanish writer born in 1927. She wrote more than 4,000 romantic novels and photonovels, and sold more than 400 million books. Her style was direct and very simple, and she was very popular in Spanish-speaking countries.

"Yes, Bernardo, I know! María Teresa is a very beautiful woman, but her beauty doesn't impress me. I can have many women like her."

Oh, gosh! I'd have died to be like María Teresa Cortés: red hair, green eyes, fair skin like marble, tall and thin, and with the natural elegance of the Spanish aristocrats. She was not only studying to become a medical doctor, but she even drove her own car at a time when driving was still unthinkable for most men. María Teresa was wealthy all right, but she was also a model of beauty, virtue, and goodness.

"What I need is her money and her family's reputation," Alfredo kept saying. "María Teresa's father is a well-known judge in Madrid, her older brother is a surgeon, and her brother-in-law has the title of Marques. What else can I ask for? With her money and family background, I could own my own clinic and work as the head physician.

"How come? You told me you have no plans to finish medical school."

"That's exactly right, my friend! I don't like studying and I have no intention of finishing my degree. That's why I need to marry María Teresa so I can to purchase my own clinic. Who would question that I am well suited to be a physician if I work in my own clinic and have well off patients willing to pay for my services?"

"How can you do this to María Teresa? This is neither honest nor ethical, and you know it."

"It's not as bad as you think. Not loving María Teresa doesn't mean that I'm not going to make her happy. She is crazy about me. It will not take much to make her happy. You'd have to see her trembling when I kiss her and hold her tight."

"But you can't pretend to love her just to get what you want!"

"Oh, yes, I can! Look at you! All your integrity and good deeds haven't been enough to make a successful physician out of you. After finishing medical school with honors you aren't more than just a rural doctor. This is not going to happen to me. You could have married Leonor Bilbao and be a renowned doctor in Madrid by now, but your pride wouldn't let you do it."

"I didn't marry Leonor because I wasn't in love with her, nor did I want her money. Besides, I remind you that I'm a rural doctor not because I'm not good enough to work in a big city but because I want to be close to my elder mother and she happens to live in a village."

What a relief for Bernardo when two years later a new physician arrived to work with him at the rural clinic, just when he had given up hope waiting for another doctor willing to work in the village.

"What is she doing here?" Bernardo asked himself in disbelief and still in shock as he approached to greet the new doctor. *"What is María Teresa doing here alone? Where is my old friend Alfredo? Why haven't they come together? Will she remember me?"*

No, María Teresa didn't remember Bernardo Irieta.

"Pleasure to meet you, doctor Irieta. I'm Doctor Cortés. I'm sure we'll work well together."

"I'm sure too, Doctor Cortés. There is too much work here for only one doctor, I am glad you came."

Why wasn't a wealthy young woman like María Teresa working in Madrid? Why had she chosen to take a post in the middle of nowhere? Where was her husband, Alfredo? He couldn't dare to ask her any of those questions, but he was dying to know.

Working alongside María Teresa became a pleasure and a torment for doctor Irieta, her presence disturbed Bernardo's senses. The movements of her body inside the white gown, her perfect smile and her fresh breath; all in María Teresa invited Bernardo to fall passionately in love. Her delicate anatomy and the firmness of her spirit captivated Bernardo's good judgment to the degree of desiring to hold her in his arms and make her tremble as she did when Alfredo kissed her. No, Bernardo couldn't do it, he had to respect his friend who was probably in Madrid awaiting her arrival.

More than a year of working together had passed when María Teresa started showing open emotions towards Bernardo, but his constant rejection made her clearly believe that he wasn't interested in her.

"I knew it!" Bernardo exclaimed one day he saw his old friend coming into the clinic.

"What are you doing here?" the astonished María Teresa asked Alfredo.

"Forgive me, María Teresa, please forgive me! I came a long way to ask you to be my wife."

"What are you talking about? Are you crazy? You are a married man!"

"My wife, Leonor Bilbao, passed away in an accident a few months ago. I don't need your money now, Leonor left me more than I need, but I desperately need your love."

"And what makes you think that I want to be your wife?"

"You always loved me, you can't deny it. I was a fool for letting you go."

"No, Alfredo. You got it all wrong! I thought I loved you, but my love for you was just an illusion. I was very young then and I fell in love with the man I thought you were, very far from the man you really are."

"I've changed, María Teresa. I am a different man now. I've made many mistakes but I want to show you the best part of the man you fell in love with years ago."

"It's too late, Alfredo. Now I know what love means, and I can assure you that it has nothing to do with what I felt for you."

"Is there another man?"

"Yes, there is another man, a real man, an honest and hardworking man, a man who has principles."

"Have you fallen in love with a peasant? Maybe a shepherd? Don't make me laugh!" Alfredo said.

"I've fallen in love with the best doctor I've ever met. This profession was just a business for you and a way to show off. For Doctor Irieta, however, it's a personal crusade to do good in the world."

"Doctor Irieta? Bernardo Irieta! My old friend Bernardo?" Alfredo exclaimed in denial.

"Have you met doctor Irieta before?"

Bernando had been listening next door with his heart pounding.

"Hello Alfredo, it's being a long time!" Bernando said entering the room.

"Bernardo! What are you doing here?"

"I'm a rural doctor, remember? This is the village where I work and I live."

"Do you know each other?" María Teresa asked.

"This is a long and boring story, my love," Bernardo said, "and we have more important things to talk about now. Will you be my wife?" he asked holding her tight and kissing her lips as he had dreamt of doing many times.

"Yes, I will!"

Mima not only brought us magazines and books from the houses of the rich, but also leftovers of dishes we had never eaten before like *gazpacho andaluz* made with a base of tomato puree and pieces of onion, green pepper, and cucumber. Or *cocido madrileño*, a heavy dish with many vegetables, garbanzo beans, and different sorts of meat like chicken, beef, or pork. We ate better than most of our neighbors.

Hand-me-downs were very much appreciated in my house. *Mima* took every piece of cloth that the wealthy didn't want and transformed it into nightgowns, dresses, jackets, coats and whatever else we needed; Mayda and I dressed better than our neighbors, and we also smelled better than everybody in the solar because we used the perfume leftovers that Mima brought in small glass containers. *Maja* and *Joya* had a mysterious blend of rose and jasmine and transported us to far away exotic places, not like the pestilent *Siete Potencias* that la Negra María used that gave us all a headache when she walked up and down the hallway of the *solar*.

Mayda and I were as poor as la Negra María and the other neighbors, but we ate better, dressed better, and smelled better than everyone else in the solar. Besides, we were the only kids who managed to go to a private school. Still, stubborn Pipo, didn't want Mima to work outside the home, "Don't you have enough to do at home that you have to go outside and clean the shit of others?"

"Give me money! Don't drink it away, and I will not have to clean other shit than yours," Mima answered.

Sometimes, she didn't bother to answer; she couldn't care less. She had always worked as a maid, and she knew it was a decent job to raise her daughters. First, when Mayda and I were little, Mima started sewing at home and took the laundry for several families and for a convent of Catholic nuns. When we were a little older, she started working in a house as a cook, and later doing the cleaning and whatever else the wealthy ladies asked her to do. She looked pretty in her maid uniform, like a nurse.

Some *señoras* were better than others. One time a *señora* took an old and greasy, dirty curtain from the kitchen and gave it to Mima saying "Here, Obdulia, for you to take home and make some clothes for your kids."

"Very pretty fabric, *señora, y*ou're very kind, thank you."

Mima never showed resentment or ingratitude to the *señoras*, not even when they reprimanded her.

"Never call me Carmen again in front of other people. For you I am *señora*, understand?"

"Yes, *señora*, it will not happen again, *señora*."

When Mima found *señora* Mendieta, the other wealthy ladies became less than a memory. She was not only the richest of the rich, *señora* Mendieta was a real lady. She treated Mima and all the other workers of her house with respect and tenderness. She also made sure that all her workers' kids were in good schools, well fed, and well dressed. Until the day *señora* Mendieta and her family left the island for good, they were family to us. They paid the largest part of our Catholic school fees, and they even paid for my parents' wedding. *Señora* Mendieta gave us confidence and security, the feeling of being part of a wealthy Spanish family.

"She is my aunt from Spain," I would tell my friends bragging, "And in Spain she has a castle where we can go and stay as much as we want, and her grandfather was a knight who wore armor and rode a white horse around his castle supervising his land and his peasants."

None of my friends ever asked me why we lived in a solar while my wealthy and noble aunt from Spain lived in one of the most incredible houses of Havana. That confidence gave me wings to fly even higher and stretch my story to the extreme.

"And Franco is the brother-in-law of my aunt," I said proud of my heritage, mentioning the name of the Spanish general I had just learned at school.

The imagination of my little neighbors was as vivid as mine, though.

"My uncle is a policeman and he would defend me if somebody beat me up at school," said the girl next door.

"And Batista is a friend of my father and he gives us whatever we want," said the boy across our house.

Chapter 2
SANTA BÁRBARA AND OCHÚN

The day Mima bought the frigidaire all the neighbors were in shock. That day marked the before and after of our lives in the *solar*. Mayda and I were crazy with excitement and the whole *solar* lived the event with astonishment. We became the heroes of the neighborhood, proud descendents of a lineage of Spanish nobility.

Mima had already become quite popular when she bought a radio on the installment plan. Neighbors would bring chairs, stools, or wood boxes to sit in the evening and listen to the popular *radionovela El derecho de nacer*[6] while Mima prepared mango juice that she sold for a *quilo* a glass, and opened the door so the neighbors who were sitting in the hallway could listen.

"Shut up!" people said when the music started and Mamá Dolores was about to reveal to Don Rafael del Junco that his blood donor, doctor Alberto Limonta, was his grandson who he ordered to be killed years ago, and who happened to be the only heir of the del Junco fortune.

It all began in a clinic where a young pregnant woman was going to have an abortion. Doctor Alberto Limonta advises her to wait until she listens to the story he is about to tell her, *El derecho de nacer*.

---

6. *El derecho de nacer*, The Right to be Born, was a famous Cuban radio play written by Félix B. Caignet in 1948. It was extraordinarily successful, and inspired several movies, soap operas, and TV series in Latin America.

María Elena, her sister Matilde, and their mother *doña* Constanza live under the constant control and surveillance of the patriarch of the family, Don Rafael del Junco. Innocent and beautiful María Elena falls in love with a passing merchant with whom she had a short but intense romantic relationship that leaves her pregnant and abandoned.

Don Rafael finds out that his honor has been stained and in order to avoid a scandal, he locks Maria Elena up in a room along with her personal black maid, María Dolores Limonta, or *Mamá* Dolores. The tyrant father orders his servants to murder the baby right after its birth, but *Mamá* Dolores takes the baby with her and runs far, far away, maintaining a life of secrecy as the baby grows older. The baby, Albertico, turns into a young boy, and the young boy into a handsome man while his real mother, not knowing anything about her son, enters a convent and becomes a nun. Nobody knows the real identity of Albertico Limonta, who has proudly kept the last name of the woman who has raised him. Alberto Limonta becomes a respected doctor, falls in love with a girl named Amelia and proposes to her, deciding not to reveal yet that Mamá Dolores is not his real mother.

"Stupid Alberto!" one neighbor complained, "Just tell Amelia that the black woman isn't your mother!"

"Go to hell, *chico*! Mamá Dolores saved Albertico's life and he isn't selfish like you, man. You would sell your own mother for a plate of lentils, but Albertico isn't like that. Thank God there are still decent people in the world," said Inés who was as black as a telephone.

"Black only for my shoes, never as my mother," the other insisted.

"Shameless bastard!"

"Come on you people; discussions later, let the rest of us listen."

After finding out that Alberto's mother is black, Amalia refuses to marry Doctor Limonta.

The tension builds when Albertico meets Cristina, an adorable young woman who happens to be the daughter of Matilde, sister of Alberto's biological mother. They fall in love not knowing they are related.

"What are they going to do now?" the neighbor in front agonized.

"They'll marry and have an abnormal child because they're blood cousins. It'll be then when they discover the truth."

"Mamá Dolores will reveal everything. She loves Albertico too much to keep such a secret from him any longer and let him marry his own cousin."

"I don't want to think what would happen if Don Rafael discovers that Albertico is his grandson."

"The old guy kills himself or kills Albertico for once and forever."

"Maria Elena is already sensing something. Don't you see that she feels a close connection with Albertico?"

"I am sure Maria Elena uncovers everything. Mother...there is only one and eventually Maria Elena will recognize her son."

One day, after Alberto donates his own blood to an old man who suffers an emergency complication at the hospital, *Mamá* Dolores decides to meet with *Don* Rafael del Junco and tell him the truth about his blood donor.

"Doctor Alberto Limonta, the man who just gave you blood to save your life is your grandson; the grandson your ordered to be killed."

"Listen!" Mima screamed, "The old guy doesn't believe it!"

"He isn't well yet. He didn't have time to recover from his illness. This can kill him. Let him recover first, *carajo*; don't you see that he could have a stroke or something?"

"He is too proud and stubborn to suffer for that."

"What about if he takes all his strength and kills Mamá Dolores right there?"

"What would you people do if something like this happened to you?"

"Just shut up and listen, *coño*!

Don Rafael hears the story from Mamá Dolores and subsequently he suffers a heart attack leaving him paralyzed and unable to speak. The romance between Cristina and Alberto becomes secondary as the story of *Don* Rafael unfolds. He feels remorse, guilt, shame for what he has done, and impotence for not being able to tell his daughter Maria Elena that Alberto is her son.

Don Rafael's physical condition, his immobility and his silence kept us all agonizing and fighting over the resolution for months, until one day Maria Elena accidentally met Mamá Dolores who dared to reveal that after she ran away with the baby, she was forced to live clandestinely for the sake of the child.

When Maria Elena and Mamá Dolores told Alberto the truth, our *solar* turned upside down. Some neighbors shed tears, others sobbed without tears, others applauded, or laughed, and we children danced with excitement.

Contrary to what we expected, Alberto wasn't happy with the confession.

"What do you expect?" Pipo said, "How can he be happy after knowing that his beloved Cristina is in fact his blood cousin?"

"They can't get married!" neighbors complained.

"I told you, if they marry, they would have an abnormal child, with two heads or something."

It was then, when a sad and repentant Matilde, who for the whole year of 1948 had been a cruel, egotistic, and selfish woman, reveals that Cristina is not her blood daughter, she was adopted when she was a baby. Cristina and Alberto were not blood related siblings after all and would be able to marry without the fear of having a two-headed offspring. At the end, *Don* Rafael recovers his speech and mobility and asks Alberto to adopt his real last name, del Junco, to which Alberto answers "No!" He would keep the last name he had ever known as his, Limonta.

Our radio not only was a symbol of familial prestige but also a control tool for Mima. In her heart, she knew that the little machine was hers and sometimes when she was listening to her favorite program, *El vaso de agua de Clavelito,* "The Glass of Water of Clavelito" and Pipo wanted to listen another station, she would say to him: *"¡Tá bueno ya, chico!* It's enough, man! Leave me alone and wait until Clavelito finishes."

And Mima would pay attention and do whatever Clavelito said in the opening of the program, the part that we would all soon have memorized:

"Pon tu pensamiento en mí
Y la mano sobre el radio
Y verás que en este momento
Mi fuerza de pensamiento
Ejercerá el bien sobre ti."[7]

Mima would put a glass of water over the radio, her hands touching the machine, concentrating on Clavelito's words.

When Mima was mad at some neighbors, or just wanted to bother Pipo she would say "Sorry, no radio today!" She did that one time when *Don* Rafael del Junco was about to speak for the first time after his heart attack, and the neighbors came imploring.

---

7. "Put your thoughts on me, and your hand over the radio, and know that right at this moment the strength of my mind is wishing you well."

"Please, Obdulia, *por tu madre*[8], don't do this to us." That evening the neighbors brought whatever they had to bribe Mima, and it worked because we all listened to the *radionovela* and my family got enough fruits and food for the rest of the week.

But the *frigidaire* was much more than El derecho de nacer, it became the heart of our household and the social center of the whole *solar*. Fifty years later, when all the Russian and the Chinese refrigerators broke and died, our old green Westinghouse was still working, preserving the food for my grandchildren.

Before Mima got the *frigidaire,* we had a *nevera,* as many neighbors did. It was a big box that kept the blocks of ice inside and cooled the food while the ice lasted. When the ice was gone, the food was gone too. In the tropics, having a cool place to store food is not a joke; it's a necessity and a luxury. With the *nevera,* Mima would spend her life searching for ice around Havana, but it was not easy, not easy at all. Sometimes, she had to go far to buy the huge pieces of ice and carry them home; when she arrived the ice was almost melted and Mima exhausted.

Our *frigidaire* developed a personality of its own when Mayda shouted "Its name is Willy!" Willy would become the witness of our food prosperity of those times. Years later, Willy would witness its emptiness and our starvation.

"Can you keep the black beans in your *frigidaire* for me, Obdulia? Can you keep this steak? Can you keep this milk pudding?"

In return for preserving our neighbors' meals, Mima got favors, presents, food, and services that we wouldn't have dreamed of having otherwise.

We all enjoyed the little luxuries that Willy and Mima provided, including Pipo.

"Obdulita, bring me a glass of cold water!"

---

8. "For the love of your mother!"

But he was never willing to give up his vices for us to have a better life, not even when we needed the money because he decided that Mayda and I would attend a private school.

"If you don't pay, you don't learn," he said, "the only education you can find in the public schools is how to get rid of lice." Yes, a private school! But with what money?

For Pipo, public schools were mostly for the very poor and the black. It was also true that the public schools were more time closed than open, and if they were open it was only for a very few hours a day. There weren't enough teachers for all the kids, maybe because the salaries were so low and teachers preferred to work in private schools with a higher pay.

Mayda and I first attended a public school, and for my second grade and Mayda's first grade, we went to *Las Dominicas*. If it hadn't been for *señora* Mendieta, Mayda and I would have never gone to the Catholic school. Going to the nuns was not only a matter of getting a better education, but also a way of achieving more prestige. *Las Dominicas* was a white middle-upper-class school; there was just a handful of black girls there, like Lazarita who was probably not poorer than Mayda and I, but we all assumed she was poorer because she was a *negrita*. The difference between Lazarita and us was that she was attending school as a charity gesture from the nuns who had a special scholarship for poor girls so their families didn't have to pay. Mayda and I were not on that scholarship program because *señora* Mendieta paid a great part of our fees. At that time I didn't care who paid, I was not poor like Lazarita and that was it.

At *Las Dominicas*, the existence of God was unquestioned, of course. He was the reason we all were where we had to be. We learned about mathematics, geometry, history, and home economics, but also about sin and temptation. I was very devoted and truly motivated and inspired to be good. Although my parents weren't married in the Church at that time, Mayda and I had been baptized when we were a few months old; my aunt Graciela,

Mima's youngest sister, hosted our baptism and became our godmother.

"If you don't baptize your babies, they'll get sick and die," she said to Mima.

Once in school, we also had our First Communion. I went to confession often because I had many sins, mostly towards Pipo. I talked back to him and sometimes I wished him dead, especially after he made me dance in front of the jerks. Some days, I couldn't bite my tongue.

"¡Me cago en tu madre!"[9] I told Pipo once.

"¡Maricón!" I insulted him another time when he took his belt and beat me.

The nuns made us pray far too much. We started with the matins before classes every morning. We prayed novenas, litanies, devotions. The litanies in Latin were hard to remember, maybe that's why I still have them in my brain:

Kyrie, eleison Kyrie, eleison.
Christe, eleison Christe, eleison.
Kyrie, eleison Kyrie, eleison.
Christe, audi nos Christe, audi nos.
Christe, exaudi nos Christe, exaudi nos.
Pater de caelis, Deus, Miserere nobis.
Fili, Redemptor mundi, Deus, miserere nobis.
Spiritus Sancte, Deus, miserere nobis.
Sancta Trinitas, unus Deus, miserere nobis.

At noon we prayed the Rosary:

"Hail Mary, full of grace, the Lord is with thee; Blessed art thou among women, and blessed is the fruit of thy womb, Jesus. Holy Mary, Mother of God, pray for us sinners, now and at the hour of our death. Amen."

---

9. "I shit on your mother!"

We all repeated like automats, "Glory be to the Father, and to the Son, and to the Holy Spirit. As it was in the beginning, is now, and ever shall be, world without end. Amen."

At home, Mima made us bless the food on the table and we also prayed to the Guardian Angel before going to bed. Mima took us to church every Sunday and was very proud of being Catholic. "In this house we are Catholic, Apostolic, and Roman," she often said; that meant that we were civilized people, with good manners, and a good education.

The nuns forced us to memorize the lives, virtues, and miracles of all the Catholic saints: St. Rose of Lima, St. Teresa of Avila, St. Martin of Porres, St. Ambrose. Ten years later, I would have to replace the biographies of the saints by the deeds of Marxist heroes, and the New Testament by the Russian dictionary.

When there was trouble at home or one of us was sick, Mima prayed a little more, but she also went to see Camita *la santera*[10], all dressed in white, or her brother Baltasar who was a *babalao*. Both of them lived in a *solar* close to ours and many nights we could hear the drums playing for the *Orishas,* their rooster clucking and crowing, and all that noise the goats and chickens made before they were sacrificed.

"You're the daughter of *Ochún*," Camita told Mima one day when she went to see her for advice, "You have to keep *Ochún* happy. On a Saturday night, dedicate a shrine to her, worship her, and invoke her for protection."

As her mother, *Ochún* would take care of Mima.

"Don't you dare Obdulia to contradict *Ochún*. She is gentle and tender," Camita said, "but she can be very choleric and vindictive if you don't pay attention to her needs."

And softly murmured:

---

[10]. Woman who practices Santería, a syncretic religion of West African and Caribbean origin, also known as Regla de Ocha. In Cuba, this religious tradition is extremely popular.

"Oh, *Ochún*, goddess of love, femininity, and the river. *Ochún*, the daughter of *Obatalá* and *Yemayá*, the sister of *Oyá* and *Obá*, the wife of *Changó* with whom she had the twins *Talako* and *Salabí*. Oh, mother, take care of your daughter Obdulia who is afflicted and seeks your help. Listen to this child who suffers, oh mother."

Without either much devotion or conviction, Mima prepared a shrine for *Ochún* across the *escaparate,* in the left corner of our house: a vase with plastic yellow flowers, a maraca, a bell made of copper, a plate with candies to please *Eleguá,* a plastic doll that, according to Camita, was the gipsy who protected Mima in times of trouble or crisis, and a picture of *la Caridad del Cobre*, the Patron Saint of Cuba.

On September 7th of that year, 1951, Camita invited us to celebrate her saint's day, also *Ochún*. Sandalwood, cheap jewels, mirrors, golden bracelets, and yellow beads were placed over the table along with the food for the *Orishas* and for the guests: yellow rice, honey, and a sacrificed neutered goat that Camita had roasted.

"Come inside, before the beings arrive!" Camita said to Mima.

"Who else is coming? There is no space for more beings, here not even for a needle to fall!" Mima asked as she entered the small room full of people chanting.

"¡Oh, vení, Oh Señor, oh vení!
Oh vení, Oh Señor a la Tierra,
Vé que linda coronación.
En coronación, en coronación
Bajan los seres,
En coronación, en coronación
Bajan los seres."[11]

---

11. "Oh, Lord come! See what a beautiful crowning. All crowned, the spirits are coming down."

Camita's Godmother prayed out loud with words no one could understand:

Oshun, oyeyeni mo.
O wa yanrin wayanrin kowo si.
Obinrin gbona, okunrin nsa.
Oshun abura-olu.
Ogbadagbada loyan.
Oye ni mo, eni ide kii su.
Gbadamuƒbadamu obinrin ko See gbamu.
Ore yeye o.
Onikii, amo-awo maro.
Yeye onikii, obalodo.
Otutu nitee.
Iya ti ko leegun, ti ko leje.
Otutu nitee.
Iya ti ko leegun, ti ko leje.
Ashe-O[12]

Camita's voice became softer as she stood in the middle of the room and started calling everybody's names, her eyes closed, her arms up invoking the higher powers.

"Obdulia!" Mima was the first.

---

12. *Ochún* who is full of understanding. Who digs sand and buries money there. The woman who seizes the road and causes men to run away. *Ochún* the river which the king cannot exhaust. One who has large robust breasts. One who has fresh palm leaves, who is never tired of wearing brass. The huge, powerful woman who cannot be attacked. Most gracious mother. Onikii, who knows the secret of cults but does not disclose them. The gracious mother, the queen of the river. One who has a cool, fresh throne. The mother who has neither bone nor blood. Legends abound about this female force, but she is to be respected on all levels. She is Olodumare's representative to remind of the love that should exist in the universe.

She looked around not knowing what to do until she heard again "Obudlia! Come my child!"

Mima went closer to Camita, standing up in the middle of the room.

"Watch your back!" Camita shouted, "You could be stabbed."

"Ask her a question, Obdulia, come on! Ask questions to the gypsy!" one person insisted.

"Yes, ask questions to the gypsy!" the others repeated.

"What should I do for Ramón to stop seeing other women?"

"I died for a man," the gypsy started talking through Camita's mouth with a hoarse but sweet voice, "I know how hard infidelity is. I came here today to protect you my child and to help you so you don't have to go through what I have gone through before you. I died for him, but I've also died to protect you and advice you in hardship."

Camita was entranced, her body shaking with convulsions.

"Caridad wants perfume! Bring perfume for Caridad!" she demanded.

Somebody quickly brought a bottle of perfume and splashed some drops over Camita's body as she kept saying:

"I died because I made the same mistake twice. Don't do that, Obdulia! Listen to me! Don't make the same mistake more than once," and she mumbled words and sentences that made no sense to Mima at all, "One commits the crime and the other takes the blame; a friend kills a friend; two people with big noses cannot kiss."

It seemed that the gypsy didn't know much about Mima's problems, but Camita promised that keeping *Ochún* content would change her luck. Something must have worked because a few months later Pipo married her in the Church, mostly for the pressure that the nuns exerted on my father to marry as Jesus commanded or otherwise we would have to attend a different school.

Baltasar, however, didn't believe that Mima's problems with Pipo would ever go away or end with just a marriage.

"I see water between you and Ramón," he said one day that Mima went to have the coconuts read, "water as big as the sea separates you two, Obdulia. There is not much you can do."

"Don't you see beer or rum instead of water?" Mima asked.

Thirty something years later, Pipo would die in *El Norte* across the sea, while Mima mourned him in Havana.

Chapter 3
NOTHING WENT BACK TO NORMAL

I was 12 years old when Colonel Batista held a coup d'etat before the elections. I didn't know what a coup d'etat was but it must have been something serious because all schools closed and Mayda and I were locked up at home, listening to the news on the radio. People had panic in their faces and I started dreaming of war almost every night. In my dreams, I saw Mima in the streets, her body destroyed by a bomb and her blood spilled on the ground, but she was still alive. I tried to reach to her but she screamed to me "run Rosita, run" and I ran and left her there, dying. I woke up soaked with sweat and urine.

We heard horrible things about Batista and his police; they killed and tortured. Many young people died just for walking out at night on the streets. At that time being a student and being young were big threats to the government and all could pay with their lives.

However, the reality was that Batista's coup didn't change our lives much; we kept having the same constant fear we had always felt. One day Mima would say: "the police have committed a massacre at the university," and another day "the rebels have attacked the Moncada Barracks," and another day "Batista has killed 50 rebels that were imprisoned." Something bad happened every day, but life remained very much the same for us. The two major events of my life during those years had nothing to do with Batista's coup or with the Moncada attack; first, at the end of 1954 I stopped urinating in bed, and second I turned fifteen in 1955 shortly after Batista won the elections and assumed once again the Presidency of the Republic of Cuba. While Batista and his followers were celebrating their victory, I celebrated *mis quince,* my fifteenth birthday. Mima meanwhile hallowed her liberation from the daily boiling of peed sheets.

Until that moment my life had been limited to the right corner of my house, behind the *escaparate*, but when in 1956 I heard *la bola,* the gossip, about the rebels who came to save the island from Batista's bloody regime, something switched my brain on. I started developing ideas of my own and became involved in the support of the rebels. I don't know exactly how it happened; I was becoming a different person; I felt blood in my veins; I felt a pulse. I felt alive. Something that had been essential in my awakening was listening to Batista on the radio announcing the death of a man named Fidel Castro after the landing of the boat *Granma* in *Oriente*. I didn't know anything about that man but I heard people saying he was a hero that had died for the poor and the peasants.

More and more people started supporting the rebels. University students held many demonstrations against Batista. There were protests at schools and strikes at the *Instituto* and at the University. I attended a private academy with aspirations to become a secretary in English and Spanish, and although the academy was not a focus of rebellion, I had friends who attended the *Instituto* and were all very involved in supporting the rebels; all their conversations were about the fighting in the *Sierra Maestra*, rebellion, tortures, and crimes.

My parents were scared to death of the police but they also thought that the rebels were a bunch of madmen. After all, they didn't want us to get involved in politics because politics meant death. Regardless of Pipo's advice, my friends Teté, Amalia, her boyfriend Neno, and I started raising money to fight against Batista. The four of us lived close by in Luyanó, and had been neighbors and friends for many years. Neno attended the University, but the University closed from 1956 to 1959, which ironically gave Neno more time to spend in conspiring against the government. For Teté and for me it was like a game, but for Amalita the game would turn into serious business.

I performed other small tasks to counter the dictatorship. I sold bonds for the anti-Batista group *Movimiento 26 de Julio* whose head was then the same Fidel Castro who apparently had not died. The Movement needed money to buy guns and uniforms. I didn't know well what we were doing but we encouraged each other to keep going; very much like friends who play together, only this time we were fighting together. *Revolución* meant for us get rid of Batista and bring back peace and justice to Cuba. Amalia and Neno worked more in the underground. They disappeared for days at the time and hid somewhere. Teté and I didn't know much about what they were doing there, they would just say: "Don't ask questions and do what we tell you, alright?" and so we did.

In 1958, I became clandestinely involved with the workers' union. The idea of being clandestine fascinated me. By then, I was working all year round in an American company, Tropical Gas. As a way to avoid giving permanent contracts, many young people worked only for five or six months after which they were fired and rehired again. The union was for us a way to fight for better working conditions. We became more and more interested in justice and workers' rights. It was exciting, invigorating, and I felt good trying to fight for fairness. At that time I didn't know that working in the union would help me later in my personal life after the triumph of the Revolution. None of us knew what was going to happen. We got involved in all those things without really thinking much about the consequences, good or bad; we were idealistic. At that time I had already read Fidel Castro's written speech <u>La historia me absolverá</u>.[13]

"There are six hundred thousand Cubans without work," he wrote.

---

[13]. *History Will Absolve Me*. A four-hour speech given in 1953 by Fidel Castro in his defense during his trial following the unsuccessful guerrilla attack on the Moncada barracks on July 26 of that year.

"Five hundred thousand farm laborers who live in miserable shacks, who work four months of the year and starve the rest, sharing their misery with their children. Four hundred thousand industrial workers and laborers whose retirement funds have been embezzled, whose benefits are being taken away, whose homes are wretched quarters, whose salaries pass from the hands of the boss to those of the moneylender, whose future is a pay reduction and dismissal, whose life is endless work and whose only rest is the grave. One hundred thousand small farmers who live and die working land that is not theirs. Thirty thousand teachers and professors who are so devoted, dedicated and so necessary to the better destiny of future generations and who are so badly treated and paid. Twenty thousand small business men weighed down by debts, ruined by the crisis and harangued by a plague of grafting and venal officials. Ten thousand young professional people: doctors, engineers, lawyers, veterinarians, school teachers, dentists, pharmacists, newspapermen, painters, sculptors, etc., who finish school with their degrees anxious to work and full of hope, only to find themselves at a dead end, all doors closed to them, and where no ears hear their clamor or supplication." This is what he wrote, so beautiful, so inspiring.

In my reading, I could hear his convincing words. I could feel his courage, his passion. I knew it, I understood it; there was only one solution for Cuba, *¡Revolución!*.

Things were getting bad, really bad. The last months before the revolutionary victory, life was chaotic in Havana. Batista's police were relentless in their persecution of the underground. The police went to Neno's house in the middle of the night and arrested him. Amalia was next. When Mayda told me, I started shaking. I threw up; I felt a flame in the middle of my chest and my brain exploded inside my head. I fainted and woke up two days later.

We didn't know what was going to happen. We heard of tortures every day. I couldn't handle my panic. I cried for days and hid behind the *escaparate* again. I lost the notion of time. There were rebellions and strikes everywhere, and I kept hiding.

One morning a neighbor came door-to-door, knocking and shouting, "He has fallen, he is gone, he is gone forever, he ran away!" There were moments of confusion, fear, and afterwards joy, so much joy. We had won!!! We couldn't believe it. Batista was gone! All the neighbors woke up, we could hear voices everywhere, but people did not feel safe yet to go outside and celebrate the victory. It could have been a lie. People had feared for their lives for so long that they couldn't overcome the fear so easily.

We turned on the radio, and Radio Venezuela confirmed the news.

"Cuba is free! Batista has gone in the middle of the night with his relatives and some of his closest friends."

The underground came out. The wounded, the tortured, and the hidden began to surface. Amalia and Neno had been tortured in prison. Amalita had also been raped and she needed immediate surgery. Teté and I went to the hospital to see her. The torture had severely damaged her liver and kidneys. Colonel Esteban Ventura Novo, the most feared of Batista's chiefs of police, the butcher of Havana, had interrogated her in person. There wasn't a person in Havana who didn't know of Ventura Novo. He used to appear on the front page of newspapers dressed in a white suit, sometimes holding a weapon as a symbol of his power. He inspired horror and repugnance for directing his aggression at young people, whatever their academic level, social class, faith or ideology; we were all guilty just for being young and potential rebels. He mutilated his victims, chopped them up, and dumped them into the sea.

"How did you manage to survive?" Teté asked.

"I took his gun! When he was asking me questions, I took his gun!" Amalia said in a soft but proud voice, "He didn't think I was capable of moving a finger and he left his gun on the table while he was interrogating me. He got distracted for a second and I found myself moving my hand faster than my mind. I got it! I got his gun and pointed it at him. I looked deep into his eyes. He looked back at me and we stared at each other in silence. I saw fear in his eyes."

Ventura Novo could be an unscrupulous murderer, but he was also a coward who did not personally stain his clothes or his hands with the blood of his victims. He supervised the work of his torture in beatings and the removing of nails but he never did that himself.

"Put the gun down!" he commanded me.

"I froze. My whole body stiffed. I felt a rush of power and a cold shiver up and down my spine."

"Put the gun down!" he shouted louder this time, "If you put the gun down, you will not be hurt. Do what I say!"

"I could have killed him right there, but I didn't do it. Why didn't I kill that bastard? I lowered the gun and put it back on the table. He quickly grabbed the gun and I thought 'It's the end for you, Amalia.' I felt the worst panic of my life. I passed out after I heard him slamming the door. I didn't see him again."

"Why didn't I kill him? Why didn't he kill me?" Amalia asked herself over and over again pulling her hair in despair. She would never forget the eyes of Ventura Novo staring at her while she pointed the gun at him. That moment of power would give her the courage to fight many other battles, more tortures, and such was her obsession that years later Amalita would follow Ventura Novo in exile to ask him why he didn't kill her.

Nothing went back to the way it was before. After Batista left the country, we celebrated, celebrated, and celebrated some more. Men, women, and children went out to the streets of Havana, crying and laughing hysterically. We kissed and hugged people we had never seen before. We congratulated one another as if all of us had won a major prize in a contest. We were all one, men and women, black and white, poor and rich; there was no division among the people back in those heady days after the victory.

I was almost nineteen when I saw *los barbudos* arriving triumphantly into Havana. I went to the *Malecón* to see them coming and I tried to walk with the crowd through *Calle 23*. "Fidel! Fidel! Fidel! Fidel!" everybody shouted. The enthusiasm was something unbelievable. Everything was black and red in the streets, the colors of the *Movimiento 26 de Julio*. We wore bracelets, and people waved flags with those colors.

Seeing *los barbudos* was the greatest thing in the world for me. There they were: Camilo Cienfuegos, Ché Guevara, Fidel Castro, and others waving and smiling. We helped them win, we helped them get rid of Batista and that was our victory too, our Revolution. We felt so much love for those *barbudos*, our heroes; they were not madmen anymore; our love for them united us all.

Mima thought that God Himself had sent Fidel Castro to the island.

"The Holy Spirit has sent him to us, Rosita," Mima said after watching how a white dove stayed on Fidel Castro's shoulder while he was giving his first speech in Havana at *Ciudad Libertad* on January 8th. Fidel had a beard and was 33 when he came into Havana, the same age as Jesus Christ when he died. Not long before that, Batista had publicly announced his death, and there he was alive and fresh from his descent from the mountains. Without a doubt, Fidel Castro was the Messiah of the Caribbean, the one who came to bring freedom and justice to the island. We were the chosen people, the people of God.

We lived those days, and the days after those days, and many more days afterwards in a state of frenzy and delirium. Our lives were on hold, nobody cared about their own business because there was just one major business: to celebrate the victory and get ready for what was about to come.

When the island was officially proclaimed a socialist country, we started with new programs and policies such as free and equal access to education and employment, affordable food, housing, and medical care. We were told that the Revolution would eventually cover all our needs: free medicines, better transportation, food for all, new employment, political freedom, freedom of religion, an increase in salaries, free beaches for everyone, no racial discrimination, no prostitution, no gambling, land reform with free peasants; what else could we hope for? Unbelievable!

Mima, Mayda, and I attended different educational programs and activities to learn about the new opportunities to help our country. In 1960, Vilma Espín, who by that time was already the wife of Fidel Castro's brother Raúl, created the Federation of Cuban Women, we called it *FMC* or just *Federación*, with the intention of integrating women in revolutionary life. The *Federación* created the Ana Betancourt schools for peasant girls and women, and Mima volunteered teaching girls how to cut fabric and sew. Thousands of women came from the countryside to Havana to get an elementary education and indoctrination into Marxism and Socialism. The selection of the girls was based on their aptitude to study and work, their self-discipline, and their desire to improve.

She also worked for a program that rehabilitated prostitutes, many of them young women with horrible stories of abuse, like Albertina, a *guajira* who started working in the streets of Havana before she turned seventeen.

"You see *doña* Obdulia," she said to Mima, "Before the Revolution, there wasn't anything I could do in the city but sell my body."

"Why didn't you work as a maid, like I did?"

"I don't know; it was my fate, I guess. I left home at a very young age. I came with a girl friend from my village to find work in Havana. We didn't realize how ignorant we were. We were not afraid of the city, although the bright lights of the night disoriented us at first. We had enough *pesos* in our pockets to survive for a week. One day during our second week in Havana, I met a man who insisted he had good work for us and I trusted him; what did we have to lose anyway? The gentleman took us to a house where a lady dressed in a red silk gown came to greet us, 'My name is Lola, and I am in charge of the twelve girls who live here.' She went through an endless list of rules and finished with 'half of what you make is mine and half is yours.' We weren't really sure if we were going to wash the floors for Lola or what. 'This house must be very clean' I thought when I learned that twelve more girls were working for Lola there, probably all washing and cleaning.

That night, one of the older girls said to us 'so, you're here to sell your bodies too?' We were afraid thinking that we would have to cut off our hands or our arms or our legs to sell them in the street for a few pesos. 'Who would want the body parts of a *guajirita*?' I wondered."

"After the first day in Lola's house, each of us saw at least ten men every night, seven days a week.

"What do you want from me?" I asked the first man who came to see me.

"I paid many pesos to be the first, honey" he said.

Then, I understood what part of my body I would have to sell in Havana. That man wasn't bad with me, he tried to be gentle, and spoke with me in a soft voice. But I was horrified and I didn't know what to do. I almost fainted when I felt his fat body on top of me, his hips pressing against mine, his lips trying to find mine, his sweaty hands opening my legs that I was trying to keep glued together. 'I'm sorry, *nena*, I have to get what I paid for,' he said. I tried to push him away but he was too heavy. I gave up, it was too late, I felt his fat finger inside of me, and something broke between my legs; I couldn't push him anymore, he jumped up and down over my stomach like a maniac, now hissing, then growling, and later screaming and crying, until the dead weight of his body fell over me. He seemed exhausted, like he was sick or something. I started getting dressed to go although I didn't know where, when he recovered his voice to say 'Hey! Don't go! I paid for the whole night.'"

Thus Albertina entered into the life. Desired or not, Albertina's life was drinking, dancing, going to parties to find customers, and the following day more of the same thing, until the Revolution came about and gave her the chance to complete the educational program and find a decent job. The government even gave her an apartment to help her start a new life.

"How could some of these women not want to be rehabilitated?" Mima asked to the organizers of the program knowing that some women had refused to join the new revolutionary life.

"If they want to be whores, let them be whores. But not here, ¡No, señor! [14] Under the tyrant, they were forced to be whores, they were the victims of a system that didn't care about women. With Fidel, these women will have to be rehabilitated or go to *El Norte* and keep working as whores."

"Lola left *pa'l Norte* as soon as she had the chance," Albertina explained. "'Nobody can tell me what to do or not do with my business; hypocrites!' people heard Lola saying when she left."

In our little free time, Mima, Mayda, and I went door-to-door recruiting women for the *Federación*.

"*Compañera*, we come on behalf of the *Federación* and it's very important that as a Cuban woman you join the struggle and become a member," we said.

Some women looked at us with suspicion, but most joined without much ado. The main duty of new members was to recruit

---

14. "No way, man!"

another five women and these in turn would recruit another five and so on. The system worked really well because soon most women in the country had been recruited as *federadas*. Those not committed to the *Federación* and to the Revolution had already left the country.

Meanwhile, I kept working as a secretary for Tropical Gas. That job gave me the confidence and self-esteem I so desperately needed. My boss valued good work and I was well compensated for my efficiency and for taking responsibility for my actions. I also learned more English there than I did at the Academy of Languages.

When Tropical Gas became nationalized, my boss asked me to go with him along with some other employees to work in *El Norte*. Before the Revolution that would have been my dream, but at that moment I said "No way, man! Not now that we are going to have a country without poverty, without sickness, without misery, and without servitude. Not now that we are going to live in the best country in the world." Although the closing of Tropical Gas hurt me deeply, I had so many other wonderful things in my head that I wasn't worried about losing my job. The Revolution would provide!

And it did! The Revolution provided. Instead of working for the Yankees, I would work for the new state and serve the Revolution. I started working for the state doing similar work as I had done before as a secretary. The meaning of work, however, had changed for me. My motivation was not to work to improve my life or my parent's lives anymore. I wanted to work for the whole society. The nation needed our hands, and in order to transform the country, we needed to transform ourselves into better people, better workers, for the benefit of all. That was the idea of *el Hombre Nuevo*[15] that Che Guevara promoted. *El Hombre Nuevo* was not selfish, he didn't think about himself, not

---

15. *El Hombre Nuevo,* or the New Man, was an archetype of the ideal person in a revolutionary context, with socialist and altruistic qualities.

even about others; *el Hombre Nuevo* had to think, work, and live for the Revolution.

I became frenetic listening to the words of Fidel and *el Che*[16]. I was enchanted by Fidel's endless rhetoric. I repeated his words and I learned his speeches by heart:

"There are those who seek to maintain the exploitation of nations by oligarchies, the exploitation of man by man, and since only force can keep man in exploitation, in submission, since only force can keep peoples in colonialism, under the economic or political domination of other peoples; the only ones that need armies, violence; and destructive weapons are those who defend oppression, exploitation of man by man, colonialism, monopolies and imperialism."

We applauded wildly, and in the morning we would ask, "Did you hear Fidel's speech?"

"Who will be against the Revolution?" Fidel shouted, "Those whose interests are not the interests of Cuba and the Cuban people. The frustrated, those who sell themselves, those who betray, all those who conceived the Revolution as a satisfaction of personal ambition, not a people's undertaking, will be against the revolution, as well as all those who wanted to continue the past."

Who wanted to be against the Revolution? Not me!

Fidel was more than a hero and more than a god; he was God himself and I worshiped him unconditionally. There was a moment when I stopped listening to what he said. I didn't care about what he said anymore but I kept watching him, fascinated, entranced. Everything he said or decided was fine with me, even when I didn't understand a word of it as after fifteen minutes I would lose track.

---

16. *El Ché* refers to the Cuban-Argentinean revolutionary and guerrilla leader Ernesto Guevara, known as *Ché* Guevara or just *El Ché*. The word is a vocative expression used colloquially in Argentina in the sense of "friend, mate, pal," etc.

Fidel had been a lawyer before the Revolution. After the Revolution, his words became law, for me and for all. Few of us really understood the implications nor the consequences of his decisions. What we understood, or wanted to understand, was that all of those changes would bring about a more prosperous and fair society. We trusted him. We didn't want to contradict him because he knew exactly what was good for us. Fidel became our father, our brother, the head of our household, the leader of our block, the chief of our workplace, and the ruler of our country. We certainly saw more of him every day than our own relatives. We turned on the TV in the morning and there was Fidel, we turned on the TV at night and there was Fidel, we changed the channel and there was Fidel also.

Fidel was taking the place of our beloved ones, the ones who stayed and those who were leaving the island, like *señora* Mendieta who left for good with her family in 1965. Her leaving broke my heart in hundred pieces. She knew I had been involved in the struggle against Batista but she said only "Be careful *mi niña*, it's dangerous out there and you can be killed." She wanted change, but her husband wasn't happy with the way the new government was handling private businesses. This affected her family, personally and professionally. That was the first of many times to come that exile would touch us.

When *señora* Medieta left, Mima started cooking for a *Círculo Infantil*, one of the new daycares the Revolution created to help working mothers. Many women like Mima started working for the state, in government facilities. At the *Círculo* where she worked, there were women who had been prostitutes, maids, and housewives in the times of capitalism.

In 1966 Mima managed to finish Sixth grade while Pipo continued his work as a janitor at the *Banco Nacional de Cuba*. The shoe factory closed. The most important change I remember was not so much the kind of job we were doing, but the sense of freedom we all felt. Suddenly, we had no bosses, neither *Señor* nor *Señora* for Mima; no more Mr. Gas, as I used to call my boss. Our only boss was Fidel, and Fidel was the government, he was the Revolution, he was all in one.

At that time, the Revolution gave us something it took me a while to realize. It provided us a dignity that we'd never had before, specially to the least prosperous Cubans. It was a rebirth. It was a dream, having such a different life and such a new country. We were told that we all were crucial for the Revolution, and that the Revolution wouldn't survive without our help, our effort, and our work. That feeling was very invigorating for my parents. They both became very active in the revolutionary process. Pipo became president of the local Committee for the Defense of the Revolution that we called *CDR* for short, and Mima president of the Work Council and organizer of the *Federación* of our block. All those titles, president of this, administrator of that, *brigadista, federada, cederista,* gave us the feeling of being in charge of something for the first time in our lives. We had a title and that title bestowed prestige and a place in the revolutionary process. Those titles dignified many women who had never been in charge of anything in their lives. We felt useful, we were doing something good for Cuba, and our efforts were acknowledged in return. We, ordinary people, felt powerful, special and exceptional.

I committed myself one hundred percent to the struggle. In 1961, the Year of Education, I volunteered for the Literacy Campaign. I went to the countryside in *Oriente*, in the middle of nowhere, to teach peasants how to read and write. There I was, a *brigadista*, with my olive-green uniform. I felt so important.

"F as Fidel and *fusil*; R as Raúl and *Revolución*," I said to the peasants.

It wasn't an easy job, but the peasants, adults and children, were so grateful that we felt at the same time important but somehow unworthy. The experience was also very eye opening. We saw how neglected the countryside had been in Cuba where peasants were still living in the Middle Ages. Of course, we were all

Cubans but they seemed to be from a different planet, alien, and centuries behind.

After seven months in *Oriente*, I came back to Havana looking forward to telling everyone my experiences as a *brigadista*. It was wonderful! Later, voluntary work would be a nightmare for me after I had my three children, but at that time it was a blessing. I was single, and that had been the first time I felt free, out of Pipo's control.

Mima had been working outside the home for years, so doing volunteer work didn't mean more freedom for her, but it meant freedom in the sense that she didn't feel she had to do it but wanted to do it; not for money, not for survival anymore, but for the sake of her country. For some married women who had been stay-at-home-moms for decades, volunteering outside the home was a dream come true.

"My husband can't say anything to me because I am working for the Revolution and Fidel is asking me to do so," they said happily.

Fidel asked parents and husbands to collaborate with the Revolution and let their daughters and wives work. For some of the neighborhood women, that freedom cost them their marriage as many men were too *machista* and unable to give up their women to the Revolution. Pipo, although he had a big mouth, let us do almost whatever we pleased, and Mima, Mayda, and I got involved in all the voluntary work possible. Learning the ideology of the Revolution was not enough; we had to put the ideology to work and that also meant learning how to avoid the mistakes of our previous capitalist life.

One part of our lives that Mayda and I had to change dramatically was our Catholic beliefs; we learned how to reject them. That was something that troubled Mima a great deal at first. For her, it didn't make any sense that Fidel, himself a Catholic, educated in a Catholic school and wearing a necklace with a cross around his neck, became a pagan all of a sudden.

"If he was sent by the Holy Spirit, what is all of this non sense about?" Mima would ask.

It didn't bother me much, however. Mayda and I understood and saw things the way they were, and not the way my parents and the nuns had told us. The whole issue of religion fell apart rapidly in our lives. All of those beliefs were no more than superstitions; Catholicism and *Santería* included.

As the Revolution changed and matured so did my own life. The Lord, *la Caridad del Cobre*, and *Ochún* vanished, and I didn't wear anymore the cross I'd gotten for my First Communion. Our ideology was so pure and sincere that no religion in the world could be better than that. Besides, I had little time to think other than for the Revolution, much less to pray. Even Sunday mornings I went to do my voluntary work. The Revolution took the place of the Church. The needs of our bodies and souls would be taken care of by the Revolution.

As I forgot about wearing my necklace with the cross, I also forgot about the movies I'd seen with Mayda and Pipo and the romantic novels by Corín Tellado I'd read behind the *escaparate*. Who could tell me that all those novels, symbols of capitalism and backwardness, would save my grandchildren from starvation twenty years later when I recovered them from a drawer and decided to trade them for whatever edible thing we could get? When there was nothing to read in Havana other than the Manual of Konstantinov and the novels of Tolstoy and Dostoyevsky, those hidden novels that Mima had brought so Mayda and I could learn how to behave as bourgeoisie *señoritas*. would become precious items to sell and rent, to such a degree that I would have my own bank of old magazines and books and have clients from all over Havana. That damned bank, however, would almost cost me an *acto de repudio*[17] in my neighborhood when somebody reported me to the authorities:

---

17. Act of Repudiation. In 1980, after more than 10,000 Cubans sought asylum at the Peruvian Embassy in less than 48 hours, the Cuban

"*Ciudadana* Rosa María Tejedor Rodriguez!" one of the three uniformed men called at the door of my house.

"Present!" I answered, knowing that the honorable title of *ciudadana* could not bring any good to me.

"We come to search your house!"

"Why?" I asked trembling.

"You are running an illicit business."

"What are you talking about?"

"It has come to the knowledge of the *CDR* that you are renting books and magazines."

"Look, *compañeros,* I have an untouchable history of militancy," I said, "but my granddaughter needs food and vitamins and I would sell my own soul to provide for her."

"Watch your mouth! We all need food. What you are doing is illegal. We are issuing you an official warning and we'll confiscate all your illegal propaganda."

"What illegal propaganda are you talking about? How can my romance novels and magazines damage the Revolution?"

"Shut up! Or you will have to deal with an *acto de repudio.*"

The three men threatened me with prosecution for "Danger to the Revolution" if I didn't cooperate.

But the 1980s and 1990s were still far away, and in the 1960s, nobody would have given me a *quilo* for all those magazines

---

government established Acts of Repudiation against those who showed any counterrevolutionary behavior. These acts consisted of large groups of citizens verbally abusing, intimidating, and sometimes physically assaulting and throwing stones and other objects at homes of Cubans considered to be counter-revolutionary.

considered subversive years later.

Yes, although I had learned how to behave as a bourgeois lady with *Corín Tellado,* the Revolution of the 1960s hated the bourgeoisie and wanted the poor to stay that way; better poor than rich. I shouldn't have to pretend to be the niece of *señora* Mendieta anymore. I should be proud of not being rich; I would have been even prouder if I were also black, but poor was enough.

In order to serve the Revolution, we needed to relearn how to live without the bourgeoisie, without the Church, and without *El Norte*. No more American way of life. The new magazines and movies showed us the way revolutionary men, women, and children should be. Kids started reading comics about the heroic actions of *Ché* Guevara and Fidel Castro in the *Sierra Maestra*. Biographies of revolutionary women like Haydée Santamaría, Vilma Espín, and Celia Sánchez were printed and reprinted; living models of virtue, servitude, and loyalty to the Revolution. No more romantic heroines but women dressed in military uniforms with a rifle ready to defend their country. The guerrilla fighter and the underground combatant became our role models.

After the assassination of *el Ché* in Bolivia in 1967, he would become the Cuban super hero per excellence and there would be no piece of literature in the country that didn't mention his heroic actions in the *Sierra*, his amazing personality, his love for equity, his honesty, and his devotion to the Cuban Revolution. There hadn't been a better and braver person in the history of humankind.

Chapter 4

DONDE DIGO "DIGO" DIGO "DIEGO" [18]

One day, Amalita came to my house as furious as could be. I hadn't seen her for a long time. I didn't understand what was going on, and why she was so angry. I repeatedly asked her, but she was so furious that she couldn't organize her thoughts into words. After a while, she abruptly said "¡Rosi, *esto se cae, esto es una mierda!*[19] I had no idea what she was talking about. "This communism Rosi, we have to do something, don't you understand? Don't you see where we're going?" Obviously I didn't understand. And she kept saying *"Esto es una mierda Rosi, esto es una mierda."*

I couldn't believe what I was hearing. My friend Amalita was determined to fight the Revolution the same way she fought the Batista Dictatorship just a few years back. "Come with me, Rosi" she said.

"I can't Amalia. I can't."

"It's important to me that you come and fight this shit with me. I need your help to distribute propaganda against communism."

"No way! Are you out of your mind?" I shouted.

"I'll do it without your help then; there're many others out there."

Counterrevolution was the biggest of all possible crimes in Revolutionary Cuba, and Amalia, my friend Amalita Salgado, would go against the Revolution! She was a counterrevolutionary!

---

18. "When I say X, I really mean Y." When people say something, they really mean something else; contradiction, change in opinion.
19. "This is going nowhere Rosi, this is crap!"

After having been tortured and raped by the Batista's police, she was back again in the underground, but this time in the opposite band! I didn't understand her at all. She was crazy!

I couldn't do it, I couldn't do it, and I wouldn't do it! None of us wanted communism, but to fight the Revolution was not in my plans either.

I tried to convince her, I told her "Look, we don't have to be communists if we don't want to be. *Por lo más sagrado de tu vida*[20], please don't be crazy. Fidel said this country would never be communist. Why don't you trust him anymore?"

"He isn't telling the truth."

"Listen to me Amalia! You fought for this and almost died defending the Revolution. Why can't you be happy with what we have?"

It was too late; she was determined to do what she thought was right.

Those were years of great confusion, a time of tension and counterrevolutionary actions against what Amalita told me was communism. We never thought about socialism when we were in the struggle, and much less about communism. We were very young and very idealistic. We wanted to end the terror that Batista had created. We needed a big change, a democracy. Why was our socialist Revolution turning into a communist one?

In some ways, I understood Amalia's fear and anger against the new political turn as we had learned that communism brought destruction and madness everywhere.

"Communists eat children," said the nuns.

"Communists are dirty, ugly and very pale; malnourished people," Pipo told us.

---

20. "By what is most sacred in your life!"

"Communists are the ones who invented hunger," others assured.

"*Comuñangas*[21] are dangerous people who hunt children and make hamburgers and jams with them," my uncle Pedro said with disgust.

After Amalita's visit I heard people in the street saying "*¡Nos jodió el comunismo, caballero!*"[22] And the biggest fear of my life began for me: fear of communism, fear of counterrevolutionary actions, fear of invasion, fear of having a war, fear of dying, fear of seeing Mima blown up by a bomb in the streets of Havana, fear of having fear.

Many people left the country in those days and many others, like Amalia, began to fight back.

"*Donde digo 'digo' digo 'Diego'.*"[23] That is what the government is doing," I heard Pipo saying, agreeing with what Amalita had said before.

While groups of people were shouting on the streets *"Cuba sí, Rusia no!"*[24] others sang *congas* welcoming Russian Marxism.

"*Somos socialistas, marxistas, leninistas. Mañana seremos tremendos comunistas.*"[25]

"*Somos socialistas, pa'lante y pa'lante, y al que no le guste que tome purgante.*"[26]

"*Somos socialistas, lo dijo el Caballo, y al que no le guste que lo parta un rayo.*"[27]

---

21. *Comuñanga,* a derogatory term to refer to a communist.
22. Oh man, communism just fucked us!
23. See Note 18
24. "Cuba yes, Russia no!"
25. "We are socialist, Marxist, Leninist. Tomorrow we'll be fabulous communists."
26. "We are socialist and go forward and forward, and if some don't like it, they might take a purgative."

Pachanga[28] and more *pachanga,* and meanwhile Amalita kept coming to the house to change the festive atmosphere into pure drama. Convinced that communism wouldn't bring democracy and freedom, she became an expert in counterrevolutionary actions. She used chemicals to start fires in the stores now owned by the state. She filled gelatin capsules with sulfuric acid that could start a fire in a few seconds. She called the capsules *fósforo vivo*[29]. Sometimes she would put *fósforo vivo* inside a ping-pong ball that ignited on contact with the air. Other times, the capsules went inside sugar packages and Amalita went to the stores to put the sugar packages inside the pockets of clothing on display racks.

One day Amalita started a fire at Flogar, the beautiful store at Galiano and San Rafael, while our friend Teté was working there.

"¡¡FÓSFORO VIVO!!" someone shouted, and everybody ran and screamed and fell to the floor.

My two best friends Teté and Amalia, who had been soul mates and used to share the same ideals, were already in two opposite bands. I wished Amalia had never told me about her counterrevolutionary actions. I couldn't tell Teté, I couldn't tell anybody. Amalita and Teté were in real danger anyway, one against the other.

Teté had started working at Flogar at the end of 1958 selling toys for Christmas. It was only a temporary job, but after Christmas the owner Florentino García hired her for the women's department. By the end of 1959, she was in charge of the whole section. When the big companies were nationalized, Florentino García left the country, but the store still had a large stock of North American products and remained open to satisfy a public that was anxious to buy whatever was available.

---

27. "We are socialists, the Horse (Fidel) said it, and if you don't like it may a lighting strike you."
28. *Pachanga,* colloquial term referring to partying and celebration.
29. Small explosives with a big impact used in counter-revolutionary actions.

There was a fever for shopping in those days. Fidel had increased the salaries and Mima who never had the chance to shop in the big department stores went wild. She waited outside for hours with the crowds until the stores opened. She went to El Encanto, Flogar, Ten Cent, and bought all the *blumers, ajustadores,* and *fajas*; that was all the feminine underwear Mayda and I could use for the rest of our lives and generations to come.

It was a time of apparent prosperity and people spent money buying for all the years they couldn't buy before. However, it was also a time of uncertainty and fear. Counterrevolutionary actions and the threat of an invasion from *El Norte* had become a part of daily life.

When *El Encanto*, Havana's most famous department store, burned down in 1961 as a result of sabotage, Teté, crying, said to me "I can't take it anymore, Rosi, I can't. Innocent people are being killed in front of me and I'll be next." She had been doing guard duty on the roof of Flogar for several weeks as a *miliciana,* a member of the newly created National Revolutionary Militia which was made up of armed workers, peasants and students. The Militia was like an extension of the *FAR* to ensure internal security but the *milicianos* had no real training with weapons. Teté just had will power and a rifle she didn't know how to use. During the day she organized the merchandise and gave orders to the girls who work for her, and two nights a week she guarded the building along with other *milicianos*. However, every evening after work she had to get tranquilizer injections so she could sleep until the next morning when her fear began again.

Amalia's secret burned inside of me when Teté came with her stories of fear. I couldn't tell her anything. Counterrevolution meant *prisión* or *paredón*. The State Security, the secret police force was everywhere. I felt panic at the thought of being interrogated about my relationship with Amalia. If they found out we'd both end up in prison. Officially, I was as guilty as Amalita since I did nothing to stop her or tell Security.

I feared Amalia's visits like hell, but I was not strong enough to tell her so to her face. I trembled when I saw her. Nothing could be kept as a secret in a *solar*; we went outside to walk and talk, but anyone could hear Amalita speaking against Fidel.

"Our people are going to the *paredón,* Rosi. Sorí Marín has been executed for contradicting Fidel's words. Fidel is executing his own men, his friends and supporters; and we're not doing anything to stop his madness," she said to me the last time I saw her. "Don't you understand what is going on?" she shouted in the middle of the street.

Why she didn't leave me alone? I had felt tremendous fear and an incredible desire to believe in the Revolution. I tried to organize my thoughts. Was the Revolution really devouring its own children? No, no, it couldn't be. Fidel had his reasons to punish those who betrayed him. Amalita had to be wrong. It had to be Batista's men and not Fidel's who went to the wall.

"*¡Paredón, paredón, paredón!*" thousands of Fidel followers screamed for justice. People said they were criminals and torturers who deserved to die. The new regime began eliminating enemies by summary executions in front of thousands of viewers; we watched them on the TV of a neighbor. The trials and executions, applauded by many and condemned by others, were held at the *Palacio de Deportes.*

"It reminds me of a Roman circus," Mayda said.

"Justice is served!" a neighbor approved.

I didn't know at the time whether Amalita was right or wrong, but I had to convince myself that socialism or communism wouldn't be as bad afterwards. Fidel was too good to even think of putting a finger on his own people. I had to trust Fidel; he was right, we Cubans had become the victims of the aggression that came from *El Norte* because *El Norte* didn't want us to progress.

"*El Norte* doesn't want hunger to end, doesn't want the peasants to have land, doesn't want illiterates to have schools, doesn't want us to raise our living standards," Fidel said, and we all believed he was right.

The next I knew about Amalita was through her mother, Mamá Pilar. She was in the street walking like a zombie. When she saw me, she looked around with a frightened expression; she could barely speak. When she was sure that nobody was listening, she said "Amalita has been sentenced to 30 years, she is in Guanabacoa. She's only twenty-two."

Poor Mamá Pilar! The imprisonment of Amalita was worse than seeing her daughter killed. If Amalita were executed, either revolutionaries or counterrevolutionaries could easily have turned her into a heroine. Being imprisoned by the Revolution was the worst of the worst; worst than a death sentence. Counterrevolutionaries were trash and their families humiliated. Amalia's parents and siblings were isolated, even their friends moved away from them; I did so too.

The Revolution was everything for us Cubans and Amalia's family was dead to our Revolution and to us all. What could be worse than being a counterrevolutionary and forced to remain in Cuba? The family wanted to stay close to Amalia, but the whole family was relocated to the province of Pinar del Río, to Sandino, a prison camp camouflaged as a city built to rehabilitate counterrevolutionaries.

When Amalia was arrested, I told Teté about the sabotage and the *fósforo vivo*. Teté couldn't believe it and asked me "Why did Amalia want to destroy all we have achieved? Was she out of her mind? After all she had suffered for the Revolution? Did she know we could have been killed too?" Teté was outraged.

It would be many years later before we would know that, after her imprisonment our friend Amalita would be brutally beaten, deprived of food for weeks, held in a dark damp chamber for days, and terrorized with mock executions every now and then; this time not by Batista's police but by the same ones she had fought with, side by side, to achieve the Revolution.

Chapter 5
LOVE AND REVOLUTION

Amalia's life didn't fit in with mine any more. I just wanted to be a good revolutionary and Amalia had chosen a different path. I became a *miliciana* like Teté, and I prepared myself to sacrifice for my country, whatever it would take.

And what it took was work, work, and more work. After my regular shift at the Ministry, I went to do voluntary work to help the Revolution: harvest coffee, cut cane, fill bottles of perfume in one factory, assemble doll parts in another, guard duty at my work place, and more guard duty in my neighborhood.

Mima and Mayda also worked tirelessly. That was our obligation as good Cubans. Fidel said it clearly, "There are two classes of citizens, the ones who work, produce, and create and the parasites who live without working or producing."

Mayda was less tormented about being the best revolutionary ever than I was. She took life in a different way, more relaxed and easier. Mayda also found a way not only to think and fantasize about love but also to seek a real love and enjoy it. In 1963, the Year of Organization, Mayda married Rolando, a good-looking young man who owned a car repair business. For a while they lived with us in the solar, and about a year later they moved in with Rolando's sister who lived in *El Cerro*.

The fact that Mayda was younger and married before I did irritated me a great deal. She was happily married while I was insanely in love with an actor twenty years older who didn't care a bit about me.

The day I met Carlos at a friend's birthday party, he didn't even look at me, but I couldn't take my eyes off him. He wasn't truly handsome, but he was very attractive, outgoing, extremely charming, and had the confidence of a mature man who knew exactly what women wanted. For two months I walked up and down Havana to see if by any chance I could meet him again somewhere, talk to him, or at least watch him from a distance. Many nights, thinking about him, I started feeling the same kind of unrest I felt years before when I had heard my parents' bed cracking and shaking and I had the same urgency for squeezing my legs really hard until an electric shock of pleasure left me breathless and motionless, and I could fall asleep

I saw Carlos at a couple of different places, and each time my heart started beating so fast and loud that I was afraid everybody would hear it.

The night I met Carlos again at Gloria's house, I felt an uncontrollable impulse towards him and had to restrain myself from jumping at him. This time he not only paid attention to me but also complimented my long black hair, my big green eyes, and my fair skin.

"Your father must be an architect," he said.

"Why is that?"

"Because you are a monument."

And I melted right there. I had a pressure inside my chest that I'd never experienced before, a knot in my throat, and a burning feeling between my legs that was almost painful. I wanted him to touch my body, feel his hands on my skin. What a sin, if the nuns could hear me!

"Come on, I'll take you home in my car," he said to me after the party. A car! He had a car! I was going to get home in his car!

He stopped the car before we got to my house, in a dark and empty street. I felt one of his hands under my skirt touching my thighs. The other hand was also busy trying to open the middle button of my white shirt. Both of his hands were busy searching everywhere, my stomach, my legs, and he was kissing me on the neck and shoulders. "Just relax," he said in a soft voice. His hands moved up and over my bra, then he slipped his hand inside the bra, stroking my breast and playing with my nipples until they hardened and got bigger in size. I wanted to do something but I was paralyzed, "Just relax," he repeated. I tried to remember what to do in such circumstances, like reviewing a lesson for a test. All I could remember was my friend Teté's advice "*Chica*, when the time comes, you just let it go and you'll know what to do." Teté had mention that one doesn't learn how to kiss, that kisses just come out naturally, but there I was trying to be natural while my whole body was stiff. I didn't learn anything like that with the Corín Tellado's novels because the couple only kissed until their lips hurt, the other stuff was left to the imagination.

Carlos was getting closer and closer. I could taste the cigarette on his breath. How could I kiss him like in the novels and the movies if I had this tightness in my throat and I couldn't move? He felt me tighten up and repeated "Just relax, don't worry, this won't hurt." I wasn't worried about him hurting me; I was worried about sinning and going to hell for the rest of eternity. He moved his hands away; then again down my stomach, slowly sliding under my panties felling the hair between my legs. I pressed my legs tight together at a moment I felt I should have opened them wide. At that point I closed my eyes for the first time since the foreplay started. I felt all the weight of Carlos body pressing against me as he pushed himself closer. I felt his lips first and then his tongue into my mouth. I turned my head away without really knowing why I was rejecting his kisses. He sucked my nipple, "That hurts!" I said. He pushed his hand between my legs and touched me. I could feel his penis pushing hard against my left side. He jumped onto me and pushed his knee between my legs, forcing me to relax although that wasn't necessary as I was just about to faint. I heard his breath going faster and I felt a shiver of panic, desire, and pleasure. He grabbed his penis and pushed it against my vagina, forcing its way inside. I had never seen, and much less felt, an erect penis before; it was huge, too big for me, as he tried to enter me several times without success; it slipped out. I felt a rush of pain into my brain and I knew then why having sex without being married was a sin that brought punishment and misery to whomever did it. He had finally penetrated me. I felt a wetness between my legs and I opened my eyes and saw something thick and dark going down my tights. "It wasn't bad at all, was it?" he said still breathing fast. "No, it wasn't bad," I managed to say while I fixed my clothes and thought about the immense sin I had just committed.

Carlos didn't fall madly in love with me. He didn't even intend to see me anymore; after that encounter, he was too busy acting in the theater and enchanting other young girls.

"Is this what it is to be a woman?" I asked myself in misery. The pain of menstruating, the pain of holding temptation, the pain of sinning, the pain of a losing virginity, the pain of falling in love and the pain of deception; and Mima said that the worst possible pain was the one of giving birth!

At that point I was certain that no other man in the world would want to be with me, much less marry me. The nuns would have never forgiven me for this, "A girl can be poor, but keeping her virginity intact makes her socially worthy," sister Maria Teresa had told us in class. Thank God, I got my period three weeks later. I'd lost my virginity but at least I didn't get pregnant.

Having lost my virginity became an obsession for me, to the degree that two years later, in 1965, the Year of Agriculture, I was filling out the forms to become a militant of the Communist Party and I wrote down that I was not a virgin. To become a *militante*, one had to be pure, innocent, and honest because the Party verified the history of all new members. Applicants had to say the truth about themselves, openly and with transparency. I had to confess! I was pretty sure that my First Communion, my Catholic school, and not being a virgin were three things the Party would hold against me. The first two, however, would be less important because I was a child and my parents had made the wrong decisions for me. For my losing my virginity, I had been ultimately responsible.

"How can you be so ignorant, Rosi!" Mayda said to me when she read my application, "When are you going to grow up? If you think you are going to hell, why don't you just burn yourself to death now and stop suffering?"

The same year I applied to be a *militante,* I met Anselmo, the man I later married. His origin was very humble, he came from a village in *Oriente,* and his parents had never taught him about Catholicism, which at that point I thought was a wonderful asset. On the other hand Anselmo was a member of *la Juventud,* very committed to serve the Communist Party and the Revolution; he fitted perfectly the stereotype of the New Cuban man.

It took a lot of courage to tell Anselmo that I had lost my virginity with Carlos.

"I don't know how to tell you this, Anselmo," I started saying my face burning with shame, "I am not the person you think I am. I hid something from you because I don't want you to be upset with me," I kept mumbling and I began to cry, "but I would understand if you don't want to see me anymore."

"You're driving me crazy, Rosi, what is it?" he said impatiently.

I finally said it! And before I finished all the excuses I had prepared, Anselmo, like my sister, started making fun of me and laugh.

"You're the best man in the whole world, Anselmo," I said, confident that no other man would laugh after finding that his fiancée was not a virgin.

Although I was not madly in love with Anselmo as I had been with Carlos, I was already twenty-five and didn't want to be a *solterona* for the rest of my life. Anselmo wasn't as attractive as the actor but he had a nice body, fair skin, black hair, and black eyes. The most important to me, besides his acceptance of my loss of virginity, was that Anselmo was a *militante* and very committed to the Revolution. Part of my obligation as a young revolutionary woman was to marry a committed man and to form a family with committed children, little *pioneros* of the new ideology. When we married, Anselmo was studying to become a doctor, a dream the Revolution made true for him.

I never thought that getting married would be so much work. It was not easy, not easy at all. I went everyday for three months to get a turn for an appointment that would give us the permit to marry at the Prado Street Palace, the only Marriage Palace that existed back then. It would have been easier to marry in the Church and Mima would have stopped complaining "Rosita, you have to bless your relationship before the eyes of God, otherwise you'll live in sin like I did for many years." Superstitions! Our relation would be blessed before the eyes of the Party, and that was more than enough.

My aunt Graciela made my wedding dress with parts of the dress I wore for my fifteen birthday party.

For our wedding, as a new bride I was allowed to go to the *Tienda de los Novios*[30], the first floor of a store called Indochina in San Rafael Boulevard. It was a dream for me. With my ration card I could purchase two bed linens, two towels, a nightgown, two pants, one bra, one pair of panties, and even nail polish. I could also buy two little coffee cups and a cooking pan. I was allowed to buy more household items, but the day I was assigned to buy them, there was nothing available.

For our honeymoon, the Revolution assigned us a room in a small hotel in Havana; that was Fidel's wedding gift for all newlyweds. But obtaining the gift was not easy either. To get those three honeymoon days, we first had to stand in a line to get inside the building and stand in another line just to get a chance to fill out the damned application. We joined the line outside the

---

30. Store for newlyweds.

building one day around 8:00 p.m. We waited there in the street for several hours and then came back the next day, waited a few more hours and came back the following day; the same process for three months. The line in the street never moved forward. After waiting in all the lines and filling out all the forms, we finally married and got our honeymoon gift. We didn't complain about the gift, although the hotel didn't have running water and we had to pull the buckets up from the street through the balcony. The toilet bowl was just for decoration because it didn't flush. After all, it was a gift and we took it as it came and enjoyed it.

It was during those three days that I fell in love with Anselmo. He allowed me to discover a part of myself that had been dormant or hidden, a pleasure that had been previously totally unknown to me. Anselmo understood all my ins and outs and paid attention to my enjoyment and satisfaction as no one else had done before. Anselmo was patient, considerate and tender. The pleasure I felt with him was long lasting and fulfilling. We made love until we both were exhausted and when we recovered we started again and again and again. Unlike my own mother, I was really married, and had no remorse or feeling of guiltiness for sinning. Marriage gave us the right to devote those nights to find the pleasures I had forbidden to my body for, many years.

When we came back from our honeymoon, we moved into Anselmo's mother's small apartment in Marianao, because the solar had been declared uninhabitable. The whole building was falling apart. Part of the *barbacoa* Pipo had built for Mayda and I collapsed, and the rest of it had to be torn down because of the rotten wood. Even though there were big cracks in the ceiling and the walls, my parents kept living there for several more months; they just wouldn't move. Where else could they go, anyway?

Days were busy working for the Revolution, and nights were intense searching our bodies in the dark; in the most intense of silences so we wouldn't wake Anselmo's youngest brother, sleeping in the bed next to us, without even a curtain as a separation. Some nights we waited until we were sure Luisito was deep asleep, other times the urgency of our desire was stronger than our patience and under the sheets we explored protuberances to suck, holes to penetrate, skin to lick until not an inch of our bodies had not been stroked, rubbed, pulled, nibbled, and kissed. When we had an orgasm, we bit each other's hands to suffocate the scream. We fell asleep in a pool of sweat and I was as happy as I had never been.

In 1966, the Year of Solidarity, a few months after Isabelita was born we managed to get an apartment in Santos Suárez. Fidel gave it sooner to us than to many others who had been waiting for many more years; this was our reward for being so involved in revolutionary life. Revolutionary commitment was key, much more than necessity. The few available houses were given to people like us, with an irreproachable story of militancy, with merits, with no religious involvement, and with no relatives who left Cuba to live in *El Norte*.

Our two-bedroom apartment was one sixth of an old house that had been abandoned by its owners when they left the island for good. At one time, it must have been a tremendously beautiful house. Three of the six apartments were already occupied; the other two would be distributed soon after we moved in.

I loved having my own house. What a shame that I had no time to enjoy it as much as I would've liked to. Between meetings of the Party, meetings of the *CDR*, meetings of the *Federación*, indoctrination for this, campaigns for that, and a full-time job, I spent most of my days and weeks and months working around Havana and beyond; there was so much to do for the Revolution!

As the president of the *Federación*, I helped many of the women on my block and from the neighborhood. There were many isolated women who had never been outside the house other than to go shopping. The committees of the *Federación* were a good way for them to socialize, organize voluntary work, and help in daycares and schools of the neighborhood. We did many beautiful things. We raised money to build daycare centers, we fought illiteracy; we helped women to be better revolutionaries. The campaign to help former prostitutes and the one to help maids look for new jobs and to obtain a better education were amazing. We also made sure that all pregnant women had regular prenatal care, and that women in their reproductive years had a yearly pap smear. We *federadas* were very committed and very helpful to other women and to the Revolution.

When I was the president of the *CDR*, I was supposed to watch out for the safety of the neighbors and the neighborhood and to report all kind of irregularities, like people having dollars. That irregularity was particularly easy to spot; were they buying something not allowed, or not affordable for most Cubans? For example, a TV or an electrical appliance only allowed to foreigners and diplomats? Was anybody buying different clothes or rolls of fabric not allowed at the time, such as blue jeans? Anselmo and I knew of people who had risked their lives using the services of diplomats or foreigners to acquire goods otherwise impossible to obtain; not us, we wouldn't do it!

Part of my responsibility was to report the names of those who acted different from the norm. For example, I had to report those people who listened to the Beatles, women who complained about the quality of the rationed food, boys and young men who had long hair, and those men of working-age who were not employed. All these things were antisocial, and they couldn't go unpunished.

Who did what and who didn't was of my concern as the president of the *CDR* and the *Federación*. Who did neighborhood watches and who didn't? Who did volunteer work and who avoided it? Which women attended the meetings of the *Federación* and which women didn't? Who attended the meetings of the *CDR* and who didn't?

Fidel said "We need to fight imperialism, we need to protect our socialism, our fatherland; we need a committee to defend this Revolution in every neighborhood, on every block, and in every house," and we did it, in our own neighborhoods and in the whole city, and in the whole country. Whenever there was the slightest danger of revolt or counterrevolution anywhere in Havana, all the *CDR*s of the district got together to control and indoctrinate the neighbors.

The most important task of the *CDR* was to watch for counterrevolutionaries. Although our district was not very problematic, we had to watch very carefully day and night, paying special attention to the neighborhood churches that needed constant surveillance, as they were believed to be a center of counterrevolution. That meant doing guard duty 24 hours a day. Women usually did guard duty from eight at night to two in the morning, but many times I stayed until five in the morning because there were no neighbors available. We watched everybody who came and went from every house. We were especially careful with people suspected of *gusanería* and counterrevolution. Indiscipline was severely punished.

Anselmo and I were also instructors of what we called *frente ideológico*. We always made sure that our block and our neighborhood lived according to the purist revolutionary ideology. People needed a lot of indoctrination at the beginning, a lot of revolutionary education. They had to learn about socialism, Marxism, and about how to make the new Cuba a safe and fair place for all of us.

That was the time when many people felt confused about communism. I was once leading a polio vaccine campaign when a mother approached me screaming "I will never allow you to inject my child with that trash to convert him into a communist." Some mothers even thought that their children would have a kind of amnesia and wouldn't remember who they were after being vaccinated. Other mothers thought that with the vaccine their children would start speaking in Russian.

Watching for counterrevolutionaries and antisocials was a heroic act that would be somehow rewarded. Denouncers got new refrigerators, radios, or other items for their homes. Sometimes, when it was necessary to keep order or to control a neighbor, the *brigadas de acción rápida* came to the house and the person was arrested. Those rapid response brigades, composed of armed civilians, had been created mostly with the intention to control dissention in every neighborhood. It wasn't easy, however, to determine what was an act of vandalism, rebellion, dissidence, or just mischievous behavior, and most often the *brigadas* treated all transgressors as dissidents and terrorized everyone indiscriminately.

The black market was always a concern for the *CDR* because it affected all of us in one way or another. Diplomats, and foreign students mostly from eastern European and African countries supplied the black market; it was severely penalized for Cubans to get what we were not supposed to get. Corruption was also controlled by the *CDR*, especially making sure that the *bodegas* distributed food in equal manner to all the neighbors of the block, and that the *bodeguero* was not cheating or taking anything for himself or for resell in the black market.

Since 1962, the Year of Planning, Fidel had provided us *la libreta*, a ration card for our most essential needs. Food was strictly and equally distributed. Most products were available at *la bodega*, some in a monthly quota, others on a set day of the week, and others came irregularly. We all got rice, milk, sugar, coffee, eggs, salt, cigarettes, and meat when available in a fixed quantity and for a fixed period of time. Tubers, vegetables, wheat flour, mayonnaise, and vinegar were distributed in fixed quotas but with no fixed time. Other products like butter, olives, and canned fruits had neither an established quota nor a fixed purchasing period.

Clothes, shoes, toiletries, and fabrics were also rationed through *la libreta*. Each family was given a number and a letter such as B-1 or M-2 and we could only buy certain products on a certain day of the month when that number came up. The numbers and the designated days for shopping were posted at the stores and written in *la libreta*.

The obligation of the *CDRs* was to control that the system worked, that nobody cheated, and that the neighbors who were suspected of black market activities received their deserved punishment, as happened with Luisa Gómez, our next-door neighbor, mother of *jimaguas,* who was buying beef somewhere at a time when it was absolutely prohibited in Cuba. Those were the days when all of us became jaundiced from eating eggs, eggs, and more eggs, but beef, no way!

During various nights of several weeks, a wonderful smell of *bisté* woke me up around three in the morning. Obviously, I wasn't the only one who smelled the frying beef.

The next meeting of the *CDR*, before Anselmo started the session, a couple of women complained, *"La compañera Luisa tiene carne de res en su casa*[31], and she is cooking it at night to hide it from us." That was it! The mess began; all the neighbors started insulting her.

"Shame on you, Luisa" one person said.

"Gusana," "undisciplined," "selfish," "counterrevolutionary," "traitor," others said.

"Attention please, just one at a time, we can't hear if you all keep shouting," Anselmo said.

We reported her case to the *Comité Central*. She was repudiated in the neighborhood. "Interesting," I thought, "Now, it seems that everyone has something bad to say about Luisa when apparently everybody loved her just before yesterday." Luisa was sent to rehabilitation in Ciego de Avila and her mother stayed with the *jimaguas* until she returned two years later. As soon as she had the chance, she got a *permuta* and exchanged her apartment for another one in a different neighborhood; she couldn't stand to live so close to the neighbors who had so cruelly accused her.

Some cases of antisocial behavior had nothing to do with the black market. One day in November, during a session of the

---

31. "Comrade Luisa has beef in her home."

Asamblea de Rendición de Cuentas, and after singing the National Anthem, *"Al combate corred, bayameses, Que la Patria os contempla orgullosa. ¡No temáis una muerte gloriosa. Que morir por la Patria es vivir!"*[32] the Delegate of the circumscription read his declaration of *Rendición de Cuentas* and opened the session for the neighbors' claims: *"Compañero delegado,"* one neighbor said, "there is a number of undesirable inhabitants at the corner of the street. I've already informed the *compañero presidente* of the *CDR* but no action has been taken yet."

"Yes!" agreed another neighbor, *"la compañera* Diana never comes to the meetings and holds suspicious meetings at her house during the weekends."

"She is a writer and likes to talk with other writers. Besides, she is not here to defend herself." said one person in her defense.

"Being a writer doesn't give her more rights; she has to attend meetings and do voluntary work as everybody else does," said another.

"Not only is she not involved in anything at all, but she's also *a tortillera* and her house is full of lesbians during the weekend," said another one.

"Do we want that sort of antisocial behavior in our neighborhood?" screamed one of the neighbors.

"Compañeros, compañeros" said the delegate, "We are already aware of this. The president of the *CDR* has already reported the anomaly to the *Comité Central* and urgent action is on the way." He concluded, *"La compañera* Diana and her women friends will go to a rehabilitation program until they are ready to admit that their behavior is a threat to our community."

When Diana left to the rehabilitation center, her apartment was sealed so she could no longer return to it.

---

32. "Hasten to battle, men of Bayamo! The fatherland looks proudly to you. Do not fear a glorious death, because to die for the fatherland is to live."

"She is not a counterrevolutionary, Rosi, and nobody knows if she is really a lesbian," a neighbor said secretly to me.

"Why didn't you do something for her and speak on her behalf?" I asked her.

"Because I would have been accused of being her lover and would be going with her wherever she goes."

We let Diana go and no one said anything on her behalf. I saw her leaving guarded by military police. She was sent to Camagüey to serve a year in an agricultural labor camp surrounded by barbed wire. At the end of that year, her antisocial behavior had been rehabilitated. She had to prove her cure before she could be incorporated again into our healthy society, which consisted of kissing a man in public and declaring that women disgusted her. But I wouldn't know all this until many years later when one of my own children almost ended up going to a camp after he let his hair grow long and the neighbors heard him chanting "*¡Cuba sí, Fidel no! ¡Cuba sí, Fidel no!*"[33]

Diana's apartment stayed sealed until a cousin of the new president of the *CDR* came from *Oriente* and occupied the apartment.

We were all observers, but we knew that we were also been observed. Many of the *CDR* meetings, and the *Federación* meetings became a battleground where watcher denounced watcher and neighbor denounced neighbor.

People became less and less interested in taking care of the neighborhood than in gossiping about others and blaming others for their antisocial behavior. In all the meetings of the *Federación* and of the Party, people began talking shamelessly about the faults of others. We acted as if we were the unique possessors of Truth, we were the good and our neighbors were the bad who needed indoctrination for their lack of discipline. Friends could become enemies in a blink of an eye.

---

33. "Cuba yes, Fidel no!"

No wonder that the day I found a *nailito* full of dollars in the ceiling lamp of my living-room I got sick to my stomach and scared to death of being discovered and sent to prison.

"I swear! I was just cleaning the lamp when I found this." I explained to Anselmo when he arrived home.

The ceiling was high and the lamp had never been cleaned since we had moved in. I managed to put one chair on top of another and *¡Mi madre!* Oh my God! I couldn't believe my eyes, a *nailito* with American money! I got so nervous, I put the *nailito* back in the lamp, took Isabelita to Mima's, and off I went to work like nothing happened.

I guessed that the *CDR* had not been very careful with the inventory of the house before the *gusanos* left. It would have been the obligation of the president of the *CDR* to report all items of value found in the house and return them to the government. That campaign was called *Frente de Recuperación de Valores del Estado* and so far had been very successful because the *gusanos* left Cuba with empty hands. With our apartment, the campaign had not been very successful, though.

"Maybe the *CDR* left the *nailito* there on purpose to see how the new residents would deal with this." I suggested.

"You're crazy, Rosi. Who would do such a thing?" Anselmo complained.

Anselmo preferred to report the case to the *CDR*. But, we thought that getting rid of the problem would be less troublesome than dealing with the interrogation of the *CDR* and of the Party. We decided to cut the bills into small pieces, throw them in the toilet and flush them down. What a nightmare! We threw in the bills, then a bucket of water, and when the pieces seemed to have disappeared, the toilet bowl fiercely spitted them back out. We threw in more and more water until we used up all we had reserved. The dollar bills were finally gone.

Chapter 6
GOOD-BYE!

"¡*Me cago en el comunismo!*"[34] Rolando said the day the government closed his modest car repair business; he swore to leave the country as soon as he could. A Spanish diplomat who had been a loyal client of Rolando's sponsored him to go to Spain. The reactions of the family were diverse.

"Why can't you take advantage of the many possibilities the Revolution is giving you here, in your own country?" Mima asked them.

"Why are you so selfish and ungrateful, Rolando. You can't take my daughter," Pipo said.

"Son, follow your instinct; it's your life," Rolando's father advised.

"If you leave, I'll kill myself," his mother threatened.

The three years waiting until they got permission to leave the country were not easy. They were not allowed to work and the government confiscated all their belongings. In 1967, the Year of the Vietnam Heroic, Mayda got pregnant and had an abortion because she had heard that having a child would stop the process and put their names automatically at the bottom of the list. Both Mayda and Rolando seemed stubborn and fearless; fearless of both the known and the unknown. When the *CDR* went to Rolando's sister house to do the inventory, Mayda threw two suitcases through the patio window and said that she had nothing for the inventory.

---

34. "I shit on communism!"

"I am living here with my sister-in-law and everything is hers. Take note of my clothes if you want but nothing else belongs to me here," she said defiantly.

To make their lives a little more interesting while they waited for their departure permission, Mayda and Rolando often went to his family's village in Pinar del Río. Often Isabelita went with them. Those trips were great for all of us because Mayda brought back things that we weren't able to find in Havana. There was plenty of food in the village and Rolando's relatives were very generous people.

"Guess what happened, Rosi!" Mayda said after they returned from one trip.

"The police stopped us to inspect the car on our way back to Havana. This time, uncle Robe gave us a whole pig leg and I wrapped it up in a blanket and carried it into the car pretending it was my sleeping baby. When the police stopped the car, Isabelita was sitting in the back close to me, resting her little head over my lap while I was still holding the sleeping swaddled raw pig leg. The police looked around and around without daring to disturb my `sleeping baby' Now, we'll have *carne de puerco* for several months."

A few more trips to Pinar del Río and at the end of 1968, Year of the Heroic Warrior, and four months after my son Pedrito was born, Mayda and her husband left the island for good. The succession of departures had begun.

"Are you sure we will see them again, Rosi?" Mima asked me crying in the airport.

"I don't know, Mima, I don't know." I answered.

I forced myself to keep going but it was not easy. Not having Mayda around was hard enough for me. It was not just losing her which bothered me but also the fact that I was the sister of a deserter, a *gusana*, a worm, an enemy of the state who had made the selfish choice to leave the Revolution. The love I felt for my sister made me understand and admire Mayda's decision; my devotion to the Revolution pushed me to resent my sister and to blame her for leaving.

"I have to move on. I have to forgive Mayda. I also have to forget about her," I said to myself.

As a way to cope with my sadness and confusion, I got more and more involved in revolutionary life. I was so busy making Revolution that my own life became very secondary. I spent my day shifts in the office at the *MINCIN* and many night shifts in committee meetings. I got my Russian refrigerator and my TV because I was nominated several times for the best worker of the year award. I also got my Russian blender, and my Russian iron, and all the furniture I had for my work at the Ministry and for my involvement in the Party. I got medals and diplomas as a "heroine of work."

Being a Party member meant for me something good and important; the Party was my sponsor, my guarantee, my way of getting more respect. However, being a militant of the Party was not easy. My responsibilities to the Revolution increased to such a degree that my own life was not much more than *Revolución*. I spent months in the countryside in the province of Havana, in towns like Güines, Bauta, Consolación, harvesting *yuca*, cleaning *malanga*, picking oranges, doing guard duty at my workplace, helping out in schools, and in my neighborhood, helping everywhere I could except in my own house.

Working my butt off didn't help my emptiness, though. I agonized waiting for news of Mayda. At the same time, when the mailman called out my name I hid and asked somebody else to get the letter for me. Getting letters from a traitor to the Revolution was not easy; I felt stigmatized, branded, confused, dying to get Mayda's letter in my hands and paranoid about what others would say or think.

Madrid, 19 of March of 1969

"It's Father's Day in Spain, Rosi. It's Father's Day and I'm away from Pipo. I've been crying all day. I feel so lonely here, Rosi, so lonely. Rolando says that it will take time to adjust living in Madrid and that I have to be patient. The other day I went to see a doctor for the first time since we came. My head felt as if it were going to explode, my back and shoulders hurt, and I hadn't eaten for a couple of days. The doctor gave me antidepressants and said that I must be terribly homesick because my body seems well and healthy; it's my mind that isn't well. I don't need antidepressants, Rosi, I need my Cuba, the sun of Havana, my family, my friends; I need you my dearest sister. It's cold in Madrid, even in March it's still cold. January and February were like hell; we have no heater in our apartment and I have to leave the oven open to heat the place at night. People say it's getting warmer, but I live in a never-ending state of internal frost.

There are no mangos in Madrid, no avocados, no black beans, no plátano macho, no guarapo, and Spaniards eat potatoes instead of rice. Rolando is happy because we can eat meat, beef and pork, several times a week. We can also eat grapes and fresh strawberries, but nothing tastes good to me, not even the turrón made of almond like the one Mima used to bring for Christmas from the Mendieta's.

Madrid seems underdeveloped to me; there are fewer cars than in Havana and the streets aren't as illuminated and bright. Besides, Spaniards smell like hell, I think they don't know the meaning of showers or baths. They have running water in their apartments but they neither drink it (they prefer cheap wine) nor use it to wash themselves. You have to see, or smell, the subway; like rotten onions.

How much I miss my niece Isabelita! I started babysitting last week. Rolando also started his job as the driver of the Spanish diplomat who helped us leave Cuba. Rolando is adjusting better than me, but I caught him crying the other day and saying with rage, '¡Me cago en el comunismo, me cago en el comunismo!' He doesn't acknowledge it, but he is also very homesick.

I'm exhausted. It's like adapting to a new culture has taken all the energy I had left. I'll try to sleep now.

Give my love to Pipo and Mima, and to my niece and nephew.

For you all the hugs and kisses in the whole world.

Your sister Mayda."

Part of my work as a revolutionary was to give children to the Revolution and educate them to love our country. *El Comandante* had said: "Our children are the Revolution, our children are the future," and in the coming and going I bore three pioneers to the revolutionary cause.

My three children were born at the González Coro Hospital, the best *materno* in Havana. It was not the hospital I had been assigned by my district, but Anselmo managed to finagle it for my three deliveries. It was the norm for the pregnant woman to stay at the hospital one month prior to the birth so doctors could monitor any abnormalities while the mother waited for her due date. That month was really my best vacation ever. Mima organized the crew: my aunts, various neighbors, some friends; there were always people willing to help and take care of everything while I was at the hospital. Anselmo was with me when Pedrito was born; by chance he was in the hospital and could see his own son coming into the world. It was not normal to have the father present, I was certainly not ready for that either. Anselmo's presence made me feel so nervous and insecure, it was as if I couldn't express all the pain I had because he was there watching what was happening. I felt more relaxed the other two times when he was not with me.

I bottle-fed my three children because I didn't have enough milk, and it seemed easier for me to bottle-feed than breast-feed. The González Coro had a milk bank that was very convenient for women like me who couldn't breast-feed their babies. After each birth, I stayed at home for two more months, which was a paid maternity leave available to women since the early 60s. It seemed, however, that I was not used to staying at home as I felt depressed and uncomfortable after all three births.

With Isa and Pedrito I had the help of Mayda and Mima and I could get everything I needed with *la libreta*: diapers, *payamas*, socks, little blankets, several crib sheets, pillow cases, cologne, baby powder, baby soap, and also a mosquito net for each. Relatives and friends had also given me hand-me-downs.

With Boris it was another story; 1970 was not a good year to be born. Mayda was far away and I had a hard time finding essential things, even *culeros* for the baby. That was the year hurricane Celia devastated part of the island. Most of all, it was the Year of the *Zafra* de los Diez Millones[35], the year when *El Comandante* demanded all the energy, time, and effort from all of us to cut the cane and produce ten million tones. Ten million Cubans cutting ten million tons of sugar cane!

The *zafra* was literally a military duty and I was one of the thousands cane cutters who became soldiers following orders from *El Comandate*.

"Every worker should act as he would in the face of an enemy attack. He should feel like a soldier in the trenches with a rifle in his hand," Fidel said.

The zafra, became a race against time, we had to cut the cane until exhaustion. Every night, after an intense work in the fields, we listened to the radio to see if we had reached the numbers expected for that time of the week. The future of Cuba was in the hands of the cane cutters, and although it was exhausting we wanted to do it for him, for Fidel, for Cuba.

---

35. "Year of the Ten Million," meaning the expectation to collect ten million tons of sugar cane in one year.

Aquello era un arroz con mango[36], the roads from Havana to the sugar plantations were constantly full of trucks and *guaguas*. Many days we spent more time in the roads than in the plantations because the traffic was jammed and the tracks couldn't move forward leaving us in the same place for hours.

What energy I had left, the *zafra* finished it all. I didn't know I was pregnant with Boris when I was selected with two other women to be in charge of a commission in one of the *centrales* to harvest the cane. For several weeks, I worked my 25-hour shift, until I finally found out that I was pregnant and I was ordered back to the MINCIN. I was very lonely at the Ministry as most people were cutting cane in the *centrales*. Havana was deserted; everybody was mobilized to work for the *zafra* to a degree that it was not easy to obtain the bare essentials in the city; even basic foods like *malanga, papa,* or *yuca* were scarce because all the farmers were involved in the *zafra* and not harvesting as usual. There was nothing in the stores. I had the money but I couldn't buy a single thing because there was nothing to buy.

I had mixed feelings about working for the *zafra*. On the one hand, I was exhausted and my family life once again abandoned. On the other hand, being involved in the cane cutting was affirming that I was a good Cuban, a good militant of the Party. Not cutting the cane was suspicious of being against the Revolution and its aims. So, although I felt tired, I was also proud of serving my country.

My cousin Alfonso was one of the few who used bad judgment to approach the *Zafra* of the Ten Million. Alfonso was an outstanding statistician and had been selected to work for the *zafra* behind the scene, as it were to see if the numbers agreed with the expectations of *El Comandante*. Alfonso took the whole thing very seriously and worked diligently for several months

---

36. A mess, like mixing rice with mango. *Arroz con mango* is a Cuban expression that means "That is a mess."

doing numbers and more numbers, until one day he dared to share his conclusions with his superiors.

"To reach the Ten Million is impossible!" he said. "The numbers don't match; we won't be able to reach the expected goals."

Nobody believed him, of course. Maybe people just pretended not to trust his estimates because they were far from the official numbers given and of course no one dared to contradict the dream of the Revolution for the *zafra*.

Alfonso wouldn't go unpunished; he was labeled untrustworthy and soon removed from his position. A few months later Alfonso was sent to teach in an elementary school outside Havana. He lost everything he had, most of all he lost his mind. Unable to work in what had been his passion, and isolated from family and friends, he felt miserable and hung himself.

As Alfonso predicted, the Ten Million tons were not reached.

After that *zafra* I couldn't handle myself anymore. Physically and mentally I was exhausted. I worked in the fields from February to June, and I gave birth to Boris in November. I was overworked, depressed, frustrated, and started questioning my role within the Revolution and within my life. I started taking tranquilizers and antidepressants, like Mayda who was far away. I couldn't do it all: mother, housekeeper, worker, integrated woman.

I had a tremendous feeling of guilt for not being a good mother to my children or a good wife to Anselmo. I felt that I neglected my children, I neglected my house, I neglected my husband and even myself. Some days I took my children to do the volunteer work, but most days I left them with Mima, with a friend, or with my neighbors. When nobody was available to take care of them, I just left them playing outside on the street until Anselmo or I came back home.

"I am going to end up in *Mazorra*[37]" I said to Mima, "Maybe if I get locked up in the mad house, I can have a good rest and some mental peace."

I couldn't take my life the way it was anymore, but what could I do? How could I change? When my children weren't sick, I took them to the *Círculo* early in the morning, at 6:30 or 7:00 am, and picked them back up around 6:00 or 7:00 pm. Unfortunately, almost every week I had at least one of them sick at home which caused me to take days off from work, or leave them with Mima, or with my mother-in-law. Anselmo was never around.

Secretly, I started admiring stay-at-home mothers. I had looked down on them before because they didn't help us make Revolution while they took advantage of the good things the Revolution provided for them. Frequently, I had bitter discussions with women neighbors and friends who stayed at home. Mima's friend Irania was one of them; she was so shameless that one time she said to me "Thank God I never needed to work."

"To hell with you, Irania!" I said to her. "It isn't thanks to God, it's thanks to the Revolution that you are not working but are having a good life."

Irania's husband had been a butcher before the Revolution and while Mima had to work her butt off as a maid, Irania managed to stay at home with her two children.

After the Revolution, Irania didn't listen to the Revolution's call for working women and decided to stay at home. She was completely unproductive and shamelessly complained for being branded, punished, and humiliated by the Revolution.

---

37. *Mazorra* is the psychiatric hospital best known in Cuba, also called Psychiatric Hospital of Havana. It was founded in 1857 to shelter elder senile black slaves who were not useful for labor. Currently it is referred by Cubans as *un infierno total,* a complete hell, and a concentration camp for mad people.

She complained for having to wait longer hours than me at the shopping line:

"You and your mother just go to the head of the line without waiting and don't even have to ask for your turn," she said, and continued "By the time I can chose, there is nothing good left and I have to make my children's clothes with the fabrics you all don't want."

It was true that the *Plan Jaba*[38] gave me the chance of not waiting in the lines as much as a non-working mother, but Irania had no idea what it was to be a working mother those days. There were many working mothers and the waiting lines were slow, so we had to wait for hours anyway. If I didn't want to wait, on my way to work I would leave my shopping list in *la bodega* and I would pick up the stuff later when I returned home. But some days *la bodega* was already closed when I returned and I couldn't pick up anything from the list having me to go home empty handed.

If the shopping wasn't easy for me, the cooking was impossible. Sorting through the bulk black beans and rice and tossing out the pebbles and bits of dirt could easily take two or three hours. Wash and peel the potatoes, the yucca, and the *malanga*; clean and prepare the fish and the meat when available, with no running water and many times with no electricity. I said to myself, "If I could only have a maid in my house to do the shopping and the cooking!" Of course that was impossible because having a maid was *contrarevolucionario*. Nobody would have agreed to be my maid anyway, so it was worthless to even think about it.

"Shame on you Rosita!" Mima said when I mentioned the possibility of hiring somebody to help me at home. "You don't need a servant, and besides I can always help you out."

---

38. The *Plan Jaba,* or Shopping Bag Plan, intended to give working women priority in the markets and *bodegas* (grocery stores), allowing them go to the front of the long lines in which people waited to purchase most goods and products.

At one point, Mima took full responsibility for the maintenance of my home, especially when I started volunteering for the *microbrigadas* helping construct houses for some fellow workers. Pipo did *los mandados* and most of the shopping at *la bodega*. Mima had always done my laundry, even after I got my Russian laundry machine. I never got used to that machine, it was harder to wash clothes with it than by hand. It broke down after a few uses anyways. Mima often did my cooking, my cleaning, and the care of my children. Pipo and Mima became my maids, so I could work for the Revolution.

After Boris was born, I had another two pregnancies that terminated in surgical abortions. I couldn't take another responsibility in my life. I had never taken the pill and was reluctant to get the IUD that we called T, inside of me. After my first abortion, I asked Anselmo if he would consider getting a vasectomy.

"Are you crazy?" he said, "You are the one who doesn't want more children."

"You're never home and can't even take care of the three you have. What am I supposed to do?" I complained.

After my second abortion, he signed the consent form for my sterilization and I got my tubes tied.

Chapter 7

MOSCÚ ROJO³⁹ AND OTHER RED PRODUCTS

The arrival of Katinka Yushchenko to Havana in 1972, the Year of Socialist Emulation, brought a breath of fresh air and renewed enthusiasm into our lives; in many ways, she replaced the emptiness Mayda left with her departure. Kati had married Anselmo's brother back in her village in Ukraine where Luisito had been conducting a two-year training in aircraft engineering. Kati was twenty-two when we met her. She was pale, almost translucent, with marble-like skin, intense bright blue eyes, and long blond braids falling over her shoulders. Isa, who was only six when Kati arrived, threw daily tantrums because she wanted Kati's hairdo; there was no way we could do miracles with Isa's black curly hair.

We all wanted to be like Katinka Yushchenko. Her energy was so contagious; her desire to bring Russian communism to the tropics was so genuine and truthful that it made us feel ashamed of ourselves for not appreciating enough what she so greatly admired in our island. Kati was always happy, never complained, and assimilated to the Cuban way amazingly fast. In a few months she had become a *federada,* a *militante* of the Communist Party, and a professor of Russian at the University of Havana. She would never speak perfect Spanish, though; her Russian accent was as thick as a pre-Revolution Cuban stew.

---

39. Red Moscow (red being the symbolic color of Communism; red as the primary color of the flag of the Soviet Union). The red star, a Communist emblem, led to such Cold War phrases as "the Red Menace" and "Red China." *Moscú rojo* was a Russian perfume, very popular in Cuba.

In 1974, the Year of the Fifteenth Anniversary of the Triumph of the Revolution, Kati and Luisito had the most beautiful *jimaguas* we had ever seen. Valentina, as pale and blond as her mother, and Vladimir as handsome and *prieto* as his father. It was as if those two babies had been predesigned and artificially created. Valentina and Vladimir became the dolls of the house, the joy and the new life that we all so desperately needed.

Katinka was invincible. I never understood how that frail body could do so many things without dying of exhaustion. She found time for everything, for her husband, for her house, for her students, for Russian tropical communism, and also for her twins. I've never had the time or the energy to sing lullabies to my children; I tried once but I fell sleep before they did.

"Mami, wake up, you didn't finish the song!" or "The story doesn't finish that way!" my little rascals would yell at me.

But Kati sat in a rocking chair with both Valentina and Vladimir on top of her, "I sing kolysanka to my babies; they vyery happy and not forget my mama in Ukraine." Kati said.

Rocking back and forth she sang a Ukrainian lullaby that moved us all to tears. That was the only time we heard her saying something in Ukrainian because Russian had always been her language.

"*Liuliu, liuliu, ia kolyshu, iak ne zasnesh to ti [tebe] lyshu; lyshu tebe pid lypkamy, sama pidu z kozakamy... Liuliu, liuliu, hoda, hoda, shchos' dytyni ne dohoda; treba ii dohodyty, yisty daty, kolysaty...*"[40]

After the mid-70s our quality of life improved, not only for the presence of Kati, Valentina, and Vladimir in our lives but also for all those products that arrived from the *CAME*, the Eastern

---

40. "Lullaby, lullaby, I am rocking you, if you don't fall asleep I will leave you; I'll leave you under the linden trees, and I'll go off with the Kozaky... Lullaby, lullaby, the baby is unhappy, it has to be made comfortable, fed and rocked."

European Communist Block. At home we had managed all right. Anselmo's patients were generous and compensated him with whatever was available to them, from food to fabrics and treats for the children. My children also got lucky when Pipo reported his stomach ulcer to the office for food control, called *OFICODA,* and got assigned an extra ration of milk, which most days he shared with his grandchildren.

Three years after Boris was born, the government distributed a new ration book. The rationed products were basically the same, but some of them became more regular, such as milk, fish, potatoes, yucca, bananas, and alcoholic and soft beverages. The government also established *mercados paralelos*, which opened up our choices somewhat. After ten years of eating the same food and of everybody having the same things, the *CAME* and the *mercados paralelos* meant a very welcome change.

The variety of products from the *CAME* was not very impressive but the quantity was astonishing. All sorts of preserves and canned foods imaginable! We had more of these things than we needed, and in a couple of years we had more than we wanted.

"*Give me bisté* with *congrí!*" Pipo shouted when he was fed up eating canned fish, canned meat and canned fruit, "I want real beef and not this Russian invention of meat in a can," he complained.

We ate the *CAME* stuff anyway, but we traded it as much as we could, though trading was difficult because nobody else wanted to eat the stuff anymore either.

At the *mercado paralelo* we could buy deodorants, cleaning supplies, and some items for the house; nothing really fancy, though. The quality was terrible, but at least it was a change and I appreciated it a great deal. The possibilities to buy goods opened up a lot in the mid-70s and we were allowed to purchase new things *por la libre*, without the ration card, but preserving the rationed products intact.

That was the time when Anselmo bought a bottle of *Moscú Rojo* for me, a perfume that came from Bulgaria or Poland. I hadn't used a perfume since Mima stopped working as a maid for the houses of the wealthy. Perfumes in Cuba, good and bad, had disappeared many years ago. *Moscú Rojo* would be the first of a series of Russian perfumes that arrived in Havana after the 70s, all of which had a very strong oriental scent.

Two times a year we could get new underwear, a pair of rubber shoes, and socks. Skirts, blouses, pants, and dresses were very difficult to get, but Mima and I knew how to sew so we made our own clothes with the fabric assigned to us.

The Revolution even gave toys to the children to celebrate the victory of the *Movimiento 26 de Julio*. When I was little, I received presents on January 5th, for the Catholic celebration of the Three Kings. The Revolution took the place of the Three Kings and distributed toys for every child on July 26th; one basic toy such as a truck or a bicycle for a boy, and a doll or a stroller for a girl, and two additional smaller toys for each.

My most miserable headache was when my children lost one of their shoes; we went nuts trying to get another pair as our ration was already spent. That happened when Boris swore he had dropped his shoe inside the *cisterna,* the water tank that was on the roof. What was that damned child doing there?

Something we were never lack of was survival strategies.

"*Compañero* Barilla," I said to the president of the *CDR*, "Is there any way you could get a pair of shoes for my Boris?"

"How do you want me to do it, Rosi?" Barilla said.

For cases like this, I always had a drawer with gifts that Anselmo brought back from his many trips to the *campo socialista* like when he went to the Czech Republic, Poland, or Russia. The quality of those things was less than desired, but they were terrific for swapping.

"I have this watch that Anselmo brought back from Hungary that we never used," I answered to Barilla.

It took time, but the problem was solved. Through the cousin of a cousin of one of Barilla's relatives, Boris got another pair of hand-me-down shoes, a little big for his feet but better than too small anyway.

We had everything we needed but the distribution was so limited that one couldn't get used to anything in particular because the next time it would be impossible to find. Often, I had *pesos* to buy what I needed but no chance to find it; the store was out for good or it wasn't our turn to buy. That was when people said joking:

"Today you have the *plan Camarioca: hay pero no te toca.*"[41]

"Tomorrow the *plan Escambray: te toca pero no hay.*"[42]

In spite of the *plan Camarioca* and the *plan Escambray,* the Revolution took good care of us. Anselmo and I had managed to create an ideal revolutionary family and in return the Revolution had given us the best of itself.

Isa, Pedrito, and Boris belonged to the Cuban Pioneers Union that we called *UPC*. From first to fourth grade, they belonged to the *Moncadistas* group of pioneers and wore the blue scarf that represented the sky of Cuba. From fifth to sixth grade they belonged to the José Martí's first level, and from seventh to ninth to the José Martí's second level and they wore the red scarf representing Cuban blood spilled during the revolutionary combat. Their slogan was *"Pioneros por el comunismo, ¡seremos como el Ché!"*[43] At the *UPC,* children learned values such as bravery, honesty, modesty, discipline, hard work, and solidarity

---

41. "There is, but it's not your turn."
42. "It's your turn but there is nothing."
43. "Pioneers for Communism: We'll Be Like *Che!*" is a slogan recited everyday by schoolchildren in Cuba during the flag ceremony. *Che* refers to the Cuban-Argentinian revolutionary Ernesto Guevara.

with all countries in the world, except with *El Norte* of course; the defense of the motherland was the ultimate learning lesson; solidarity with *El Norte* would mean the destruction of the principles of the *UPC*.

As good pioneers, my kids wore their scarves with pride and learned how to defend socialism by all means. Reporting deviations of friends and repudiating imperialism were expected from them. For their good revolutionary behavior, our *CDR* recommended them for the *semi-internado* program in elementary school, which was terrific because they didn't have to come back home for lunch and Mima could have a little freedom and peace of mind until the evening.

When my children reached fourteen, they became members of the Young Communist Union, the *Juventud* or *UJC*, and they attended cultural events and went on educational trips. As an ongoing part of their indoctrination, they kept studying revolutionary heroes and martyrs. The *Juventud* also enlisted the three of them in agricultural work on weekends.

Anselmo and I had been exemplary revolutionaries, good role models for our children. Anselmo went all around the world to volunteer as a medical doctor in internationalist campaigns. That was a great honor and a great service to the Revolution, and at the same time it was very beneficial for us. The many months that Anselmo was overseas, I kept receiving his ration from *la libreta* so we managed even better in terms of quantity of food and with the surplus of rice, sugar, or tobacco I could trade it for something else I wanted. Our revolutionary status also increased with Anslemo's campaigns; it was a career advancement and an increase in our family's status and prestige. In those trips, Anselmo managed to bring home treats for the children not available in Cuba, all sorts of presents for them and even things for the house, like toilet paper and towels from the hotels, silverware from the plane and much more.

Life was good, as good as it could be; but it wasn't an easy life, nevertheless. My children were well fed, and had a good education and good doctors, but I felt guilty about not being a good mother; I had raised my children by remote control. I hadn't seen them grow and I hadn't taken care of them. The government had educated them, fed them, and dressed them, and when they needed a mother it was Mima who had been there for them, not me.

The long separations from Anselmo were also hard for me. Every time Anselmo left the country it was a time of anxiety and more depression, thinking that he wouldn't come back alive. Unfortunately the time Anselmo and I had spent together under the same roof since we married had been minimum. There was always a reason for not being together–internationalist campaigns in Angola, Ethiopia, Namibia, Nicaragua; education and indoctrination in the Soviet Union; long meetings of the Party; voluntary work outside Havana, and even when we went to the countryside together to do voluntary agricultural work in the fields, we had to live in different camps segregated by gender; I lived in the women's camp and Anselmo in the men's.

My depression became chronic and I couldn't live without my *meprobamato* pills. I tried not to think much, not that I had much time to do so but when I did, I felt lonely, frustrated, overworked, and overwhelmed.

Chapter 8
THE SEA INSIDE

"This is the day that I leave Cuba!" Pipo said firmly one morning of July of 1980, when Rolando came back from *El Norte* to take his sister and whoever else wanted to join the Mariel boatlift.

It all started two years before, in 1978, the Year of the 11th Festival, when Mayda's visit turned our lives upside down.

"Those Cubans who left the island are still part of our Cuban family and we'll welcome them back home!" *El Comandante* had said at the beginning of that year.

Just like that, relationships that had been condemned for many years would be not only allowed but also encouraged and supported by the same Revolution that had strictly prohibited them before.

It maybe started even earlier, in 1975, the Year of the First Congress, with the death of General Franco in Spain.

Madrid, 24 of December, 1975

"My much loved sister Rosi, Merry Christmas! I know that you can't celebrate the holidays and have heard that decorating Christmas trees have been prohibited in the island. I love this time of the year, though; it reminds me when we were little and Mima bought a little plastic tree that we decorated with lights and colorful garlands. The tree was tacky all right but the Nativity was very beautiful with all the shepherds and the 'Los Tres Magos'[44] *getting closer and closer to baby Jesus until January 5th.*

---

44. The Three Kings, or The Three Wise Men.

We'll be leaving Madrid soon, Rosi, as soon as we get the paperwork complete to go to the United States. General Franco died a month ago and Rolando is suspicious that Spain may turn communist. There will be elections soon but the communist party is getting stronger after many years in the underground. We get chills when we think of another Fidel Castro taking over here. Cuban men often get together to discuss the political situation in Spain while the women make guava and mango pastries and take care of the children. In El Corte Inglés[45] we can now buy preserves of the most exotic fruits you can imagine; they've even started selling small bags of black beans, very expensive though. This is the life of exiles, I guess, just when we are getting used to a place we have to move to another one, running away, always running away.

My daughter Merceditas looks very much like Isabelita at two. Our desire is that Merceditas turns three in the United States, in a free country, far from socialism and very far away from communism. Rolando has family and friends in Florida and most probably we'll end up living there for a while.

I'll write you soon.

My love for all of you.

Mayda"

Ten years had passed since my *gusana* sister left, and during those long ten years all my children heard about *gusanos* was "bad people, traitors, deserters, enemies of the state;" we should forget that those *gusanos* had ever existed and if we still had any feelings for them, it should be of hatred not love.

No wonder why my children reacted so bitterly.

"Doesn't your sister know that we don't want her here?" Pedrito asked after hearing that his aunt was about to come to visit us.

---

[45]. One of the most popular department stores in Spain.

"If she stays here, I am leaving," Isa said.

"You can't force me to love her," complained Boris.

And Kati reminded us, "She not comooneest, we comooneest!"

At home, we seldom talked about Mayda; for Mima and Pipo it was too painful, and for Anselmo and me, it was a source of quarrels that we consciously avoided.

"Fuck your sister!" Anselmo would say angrily when the name of Mayda came out, "She couldn't wait to join the imperialists and betray her country."

During Mayda's two-week stay in Havana, Anselmo witnessed disconcertedly how my *gusana* sister was being transformed from a traitor and dirty worm into a hero and a butterfly. Our neighbors and relatives all wanted to see her, all wanted to talk to her. Having lived in Spain and in *El Norte* had given her a glamour that none of us had for staying in Cuba.

"You look gorgeous" some said.

"*El Norte* doesn't treat you bad at all," others commented.

Everybody wanted to interrogate Mayda about *El Norte*. In Cuba, we had learned that all countries around the world, especially *El Norte,* dehumanized people turning decent citizens into wicked and malevolent creatures. The socialist countries were the exception, which developed their citizens into super-humans and super-heroes; among all the socialist countries, Cuba was the best, though.

They all seemed astonished listening to the stories of Mayda, that woman who had lived in the evil empire and came back to the land of justice for all.

"How many *blumers* can you buy with the ration card?" Mima asked the first.

"Are there any drug dealers in the street where you live?" my neighbor Angelina followed.

"Do Yankee dogs eat black people alive?" a *mulata* neighbor asked.

"Why does imperialism turn people into vicious and cruel beings?" asked Pipo's brother, my uncle Miguel.

"*Tía,* have you seen any street shooting in *El Norte*?" Pedrito asked.

"Are you still a deserter, *tía*?" asked Boris.

"Is it true that children go barefoot and eat food from garbage containers?" Isabelita asked her.

We didn't understand why she laughed at all those questions.

Mayda told us stories about a world that was totally unknown to us.

"We work hard to get what we want," she said, "but we are free to choose where we go, what we do, what we wear, what we buy, what we eat, and where we live," she finished.

My sister did not only bring stories we hadn't heard before but also gifts for all of us: a coffee pot for Mima, toys and clothes for my children, electric shavers and after shave for Pipo and Anselmo, and soap and perfumes for me. And she brought dollars, many dollars. ¡*Caballero*! When I saw the bills, I felt sick to my stomach thinking of Anselmo and I cutting the bills and flushing them down the toilet.

If my *mariposa* sister had not won our trust and admiration with her stories, she obtained them with her dollar bills. The third day of her stay in Havana, she went to the *diplotienda* and bought a sewing machine for Mima, a fan for our aunt Estrella, and a Soviet color TV for all of us. She even bought a small radio-cassette for Kati to play Ukrainian songs to Valentina and Vladimir.

"Why can't I go to the *diplo* but Mayda can?" I thought.

"I want to go to *El Norte*, Mami," Isabelita said, "Merceditas won't have to go the fields to pick tomatoes with her school; it's not fair."

"She is not a deserter," Boris said convinced.

"Mayda not comooneest but vyery gwood." Kati said a little confused.

"Maybe imperialism isn't much worse than communism," Pedrito said.

"I am leaving as soon as I have the chance!" Rolando's sister announced.

"Listen, children," I said, "you must have faith in Fidel. Maybe we are just coming out of the first stage of socialism and when we overcome this first phase and reach the real communism we'll be able to buy food and clothes without the ration card, and travel inside and outside the island, or at least take the *guagua* without being squashed to death," I said sadly.

Anselmo didn't say much; he'd heard Mayda's stories in silence and with an expression on his face that anticipated something I couldn't foresee.

When Mayda and Merceditas left, we all felt disoriented. The whole year of 1979, Year of the 20th Anniversary of the Victory, went by like a sigh, Mima cried more often, Pipo didn't play dominoes anymore, Anselmo was sent to Nicaragua, and I felt more tormented than usual. That was the year after Mayda came back to Havana; soon, however, we would remember it as the year before Pipo left the island for good.

It was April of 1980, the Year of the Second Congress, when we heard through *Radio Bemba:* "A mini van with three people has crashed into the wall of the Peruvian Embassy."

"Criminals, drug addicts, prostitutes!" shouted Manríquez, the president of our *CDR* at the time, when two days later we found out that more than 10,000 people crowded in the embassy seeking asylum; there were people even on the top of the trees.

"Ungrateful, parasites, garbage, shameless!" people yelled in the streets.

"¡Escoria!" *El Comandante* condemned.

A week after, the <u>Granma</u> newspaper had a small article mentioning that all who wanted could leave the country from the Mariel port. Rolando's sister Marta and her husband Jorgito came that night with the newspaper in hand and asked us if we would be interested in joining them.

"Are you crazy? Why would we want to leave?" I asked. "This is a big offense to the Revolution and now more than ever the Revolution needs our support!"

"Do as you please, Rosi," he said, "I can't take it anymore. I called Rolando one hour ago and he is making plans to come in a boat to pick us up. I thought you should know. Besides, Rolando asked me to tell you too."

"But, Fidel won't make it easy for anybody to leave like this, you know that, and much less for you; you are a member of the Party!"

"I know! This is not an easy decision for me, but we made our minds and we're all leaving as soon as we can."

I was astonished, "Good luck!" I said in a hoarse voice because I almost couldn't speak.

"Please, we ask for your discretion; you can't tell anybody," Marta finished as they were leaving to see Mima and Pipo to explain the situation and say goodbye.

Meanwhile, Fidel demanded from our *CDRs* to organize *actos de repudio* and street rallies in which supporters of the Revolution turned against the scum who wanted to leave the country. There were demonstrations everywhere; thousands of people went to the Peruvian Embassy, to Revolution Square, to the U.S. Interest

Section. We had to show Cuba's repulsion for the criminals, the drug addicts, the prostitutes, and the antisocials who were leaving.

"I am going to live with Mayda before I die," Pipo said to Mima, trembling after hearing that Jorgito and Marta were leaving.

Mima nodded her head and said with determination, "You go; I stay!"

I felt ill and threw up when Mima told me the news.

"You can't do that, Pipo! You can't leave us here. We all need you here."

"Your sister needs me too. Don't make it harder for me, Rosi. You have your *mamá* here with you. Let me go with your sister."

Fear, sadness, confusion, desperation, I felt it all at the same time. For the first time in my life I understood how difficult it had been for Pipo to be separated from Mayda. I also understood that nothing in the world could destroy the love we all felt for one another. I hugged Pipo, I kissed him, and hugged him more.

I had to keep going as the situation demanded support and militancy. I felt like an automaton. I took tomatoes and eggs and went to the street to join the mass of demonstrators; we all shouted, "Let's get them! Let's beat the scum!" People threw stones at the houses of those who were leaving; windows were broken and doors were knocked down. I saw a man being dragged through the streets. I saw hatred as I'd never witnessed it before.

I threw my tomatoes and eggs with anger as I cried my soul out and shouted again and again "*¡Maricones! ¡Hijos de puta!*"[46] I was burning with fever and delirium and couldn't remember what I was doing there. I forgot whether I was attacking or defending. I wasn't sure who I was insulting; the ones who were leaving or those who were staying. I opened my way through the crowd and

---

46. "Fags, son of a bitch!"

went home. I slept for four days until I heard the voice of Mima calling, "Rosi! The police came to take your papá to Mariel!"

Pipo went pale as a policewoman interrogated him with disgust and disrespect.

"Scum like you deserve to live in the dirt, you don't need anything at all for your trip," she spat while she confiscated all of Pipo's belongings, including the garage apartment where they had been living for the past ten years.

Manríquez, the president of the *CDR* at the time, was there too.

"*Compañera*" he said to the officer, "This man is not a traitor, he's been involved in the Revolution as much as you and me."

Mima started crying as Manríquez continued, "this man wants to spend the rest of his life with his daughter wherever she is, and she happens to be in *El Norte*. Treat him with respect; he could be your father."

The 6th of July, Rolando came in a small boat to take Marta, Jorgito, and their ten-year-old son. Along with them went Pipo and my cousin Nené to *El Norte*. They departed from Mariel the 17th of July of 1980[47].

---

47. The Mariel Port is the nearest Cuban port to the United States. The Mariel boatlift refers to what was considered the Cuban exodus of 1980. Approximately 125,000 people left Cuba from Mariel to the United States; those involved in the boatlift became known as "*Marielitos*".

Chapter 9

READING ORWELL IN HAVANA

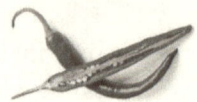

The birth of Camila brought me unanticipated joy when I needed it most because the return of Mayda to Havana and Pipo's departure in *El Mariel* had left me empty, exhausted, and frustrated.

"Another accident!" Mima shouted after hearing that Isabelita became pregnant while attending *la beca*, "it must run in the family" she said.

"What accident and what family are you talking about, *abuela*? I knew what I was doing. None of my friends are virgins, why should I be? Besides, having a child is not the end of the world, is it?" Isabelita said shamelessly.

"You have to take it out, Isa; an abortion is not a big deal, I had two and here I am. You just feel a cramp and there it goes, problem solved!

"No way, *Mami*, I love Tomás and this is not a problem we have to solve. We'll take care of this baby."

After so much pressure from everyone, Isa decided to have a cycle regulation, as we called it. Calling it "regulation" instead of abortion made it easier for her to go to the González Coro Hospital to end her pregnancy. We waited several hours standing in a line to get inside, then more hours in the waiting room once inside, until finally we heard Isa's name.

"Get undressed from the waist down, honey," the nurse requested.

Isa laid down on a bed close to another two women who were having their regulation at the same time. When Isa heard the vacuum and saw the doctor vacuuming the insides of a young woman, she started crying and shaking.

"You're such a chicken, darling!" the nurse said upset seeing that Isa was getting dressed and ready to leave the room, "Are you going to carry to term an unwanted baby only because you are scared?" We left, and seven months later my granddaughter Camila came to this world. In less than two years Isa had conceived, married, gave birth, and divorced; and all of that when she was only seventeen, what a record!

Tomás was also seventeen when they married; they both lived with us. After Camila was born, Isa went back to school and Tomás moved back with his mother. Isa finished her last year at *la beca,* and started studying psychology at the University of Havana while Mima and I became the caretakers of Camila.

I drooled with that baby, something that hadn't happened with my own children. I didn't have to give Camila to the Revolution. On the contrary, Isa had given Camila to me and she became the apple of my eyes. I was so attached to her that I couldn't stay away from home for more than a few hours. She became my safety net, and thanks to her I didn't end up in a mental institution.

Camila was with me when my old and almost forgotten friend Amalita appeared at the door of my house. It was at the end of 1985, Year of the Third Congress, and Amalita had been released from the women's prison and decided to pay a visit to me before going into exile. She had lost the cinnamon color of her skin, the light of her green eyes that were now like dark caves, and her thick brown hair had turned thin and gray. More than pale and skinny, she looked transparent to me. Her presence left me absolutely perplexed and close to a nervous breakdown.

"You've been brainwashed, Rosi. You've become a dummy at the service of a demagogue and the most incredible thing is that you're happy about it," Amalita said. "I told you many years ago that you would end up speaking in Russian and defending communism, and that's what you've done. You've become a puppet of the Party and of the Revolution. Look around and tell me what you've gotten in return for your years of sacrifice."

"My children have education, medical attention, and three meals a day," I said defensively.

"Didn't you and your sister Mayda have that as well when you were growing up?"

"Yes! We did, but it wasn't the same," I answered nervously. "We got all of that thanks to *señora* Mendieta. It wasn't our right to have it, it was just her charity."

"Besides," I said, "Now, I also have government recognition for my work. I have been nominated as the best employee of the year, a heroine of work, and most dedicated Party member. I also have diplomas for outstanding *cederista* and as remarkable *federada*."

"You've been poisoned, Rosi. I feel pity for you. I've spent twenty years of my life disoriented in a dark and pestilent cell, but I see that you have lived in a dark and pestilent state of mind. You all live in a cell and you all have the same prison officer named Fidel!"

"You have no right to talk to me like that," I said feeling paralyzed when I heard Fidel's name in her mouth. "You don't understand, Amalia. You haven't been here everyday fighting for the Revolution. You have no idea what it means to be a revolutionary, and you don't know Fidel," I said with a low voice and looking around in fear of neighbors hearing our conversation.

"You are the one who doesn't understand what it means to be a revolutionary," Amalia's voice didn't get any lower. "I gave my life defending a Revolution that turned out to be a big lie, that didn't exist, a Revolution that has devoured its own children. Because I was a revolutionary I've been in isolation cells, deprived of food, water, and light; I've spent twenty something hours listening to loud music until I pulled my hair out; sometimes I was exposed to intense darkness for days and I thought I was already dead; other times I was exposed to a white light so I couldn't sleep until I fainted. I've been punished all my life for being a revolutionary. When my mattress was removed from my cell, I slept on the floor, and if I complained I was left alone naked until I begged to be covered. Don't you think that's enough understanding of what revolutionary means?"

"Shut up, Amalia! That's enough," I shouted, "I didn't ask you to come. Besides, I'll be in big trouble if people know you are here with me."

"Days became weeks and weeks became months. First, Guanabacoa, later Guanajay. While you were here serving the Russian communism, cockroaches were crawling all over me in the dark of my cell, feeding themselves with the thick crust of sweat, dust, menstrual blood, feces, vomit, and diarrhea off my body."

Amalia kept talking, spitting all the bitterness she had accumulated in her guts, "My parents lost their jobs and their house. They have lived under constant surveillance and harassment. My siblings have been intimidated since I got incarcerated and now we are all forced to go into exile. Isn't that enough of a price for being a revolutionary?"

"I don't know what to tell you, Amalia. I haven't written the history. I have three children and a granddaughter and all I want is to live in peace."

"What happened to you has been worse than what happened to me, Rosi" she said, continuing, "I was deprived of physical freedom, but you've been deprived of your ideas and your free will. You echo the voice of your master because you've been deprived of your own. The Island will sink and you all will happily sink with it!" Amalita said angrily.

When Amalia left, I had a knot in my stomach and my head was spinning. I looked around as she had told me to do, and I burst into tears. I was alone with baby Camila; I took her in my arms and held her tight to my chest, as if protecting myself from an unknown harm. I looked around again; I saw the walls of what many years ago seemed to have been a yellow painting. I saw a Russian refrigerator that had only worked for about two years and which we used as a closet for Camila. I saw a broken rocking chair semi-fixed by Boris; I saw a Russian television set and I heard in my head the voice of Pedrito saying *"¡Se jodió el televisor!"* [48] I saw a Russian washing machine that stopped working before I could even use it, a Russian blender that lost a blade on its way to Cuba, and a Russian fan that, accustomed to the cold of the steppe, had never helped with the heat of the tropics.

I went to the bathroom and I saw the rusted bathtub as I had never seen it before. I opened the faucet, no water; Oh, I remembered that water came later in the day, at 6:00pm. I flushed the toilet, how could I forget that we needed to use a bucket to fill up the water tank? I went to the bedrooms. I had never noticed how small those two bedrooms were; a portrait of *Che* on one wall, a portrait of Fidel in his olive green uniform on another. Seven or eight people had rested there, made love, and slept in the three tiny beds we had. Why haven't we built a *barbacoa*?

"Life is good! My children have free education and free medical care!" I repeated myself, "life is good, and you have to keep going, Rosi, keep going, keep going!" I repeated crying and holding Camila tight. "There is no crime here, there is no violence, there are no drugs; life is good, life is better than in the rest of the world," I kept saying to myself, "the world is evil, Cuba is the greatest place on earth; life here is good, Rosi, and your granddaughter Camila is here with you."

That was the time when *El Comandante* called for a reexamination of our patterns of behavior that according to him were damaging socialism on the island.

"We must correct the errors and negative tendencies that have affected all spheres of our society," he said, and in 1986, the Year of the 30th Anniversary of the *Granma* landing. The

---

48. "The TV just got fucked up!"

reexamination plan began, although I had started reexamining myself already, but maybe not in the way *El Comandante* intended.

It seemed that many people had started their own reexamination process. The discontent of the whole population was rising daily. Many people were forgetting the enthusiasm and the altruism of the first years. People began demanding material incentives for their work instead of moral indoctrination in the face of food becoming scarcer and more expensive. We got restrictions in the rationed foodstuffs. Farmers markets were the only choice we had to supply our meals with a little variety, but the farmers charged prices for their products that most of us couldn't afford.

"What are we working for?" people asked, "What are we getting in return for our work?" "We can't eat just with ideology!" I heard people say for the first time since the Revolution began.

Bus fares went up while the transportation services were still dreadful; the number of buses on the road was even reduced.

"We do this so people can get more exercise to help offset our sedentary lifestyle and ward off obesity!" the National Assembly declared.

"Then give us shoes to walk!" some dared to demand.

People started losing faith and losing interest in going to work and in volunteering their time to the Revolution; it was too much hassle to go to work just for a moral incentive.

That was exactly what the new plan of *Rectificación de Errores y Tendencias Negativas*[49] consisted of: combating

---

49. Rectification of Errors and Negative Tendencies. 1986, the Cuban government launched a campaign to "rectify errors and negative tendencies" stressing the values of the communism of the 1960s such as moral incentive, the expansion of the state's role in the economy, and collective and voluntary work.

corruption, fighting work absenteeism, and battling material incentive.

What some people saw as discontent, others saw as undisciplined behavior. According to the former, the discontent was the result of many years of socialism without any real improvement in daily life. According to the later and to the Party, the unrest was a symptom that people needed more socialist indoctrination and that socialism should be stronger and more perfect than ever before.

In any case, undisciplined or not, we wouldn't be like the Russians who opened the door to capitalism; Fidel was very clear on that, "We won't have *Perestroika*[50] here," he said. The Party prohibited once again all kinds of small private enterprises that had been a source of material compensation for some and that had destabilized the socialist system; the farmers market, among other small businesses, was banned.

My own package of rectification of mistakes and negative tendencies began with Anselmo the day my family doctor sent me to the González Coro to treat an anomaly I had down there in my private parts. I waited outside in line for three hours until I could get the chance to get inside.

"Why are you here, *compañera*?" a lady in line asked another one behind her. I turned my face in the other direction avoiding her asking me the same question.

"To treat my *condiloma*," the lady answered, "I've been coming for quite a while to burn the warts. And you? I haven't seen you around, are you new here?

"This is my second week, also to treat my *condiloma*. How did you get it?"

---

50. A Soviet political reformation movement of the 1980s (1986). Perestroika was widely associated with leader Mikhail Gorbachev and his policy reform aimed at **"restructuring"** the Soviet political and economic system.

"My husband died in an internationalist campaign in Angola five years ago and since then I haven't had a sexual relationship. A few months ago my doctor told me that I had vaginal warts and that they must have been sexually transmitted. Now, you tell me how you think I got the dammed warts?"

"*Te pegó los tarros,*"[51] another lady in the line added quickly like answering a test question.

"Did you know that he was unfaithful?" Asked another one. The line was getting more and more animated with the conversation.

"Of course not! After his death I mourned that son of a bitch day and night."

"And now?" I dared to ask.

"Number 12!" the nurse called and I couldn't wait for the answer.

"My turn," I said.

Inside the room, two other women were being examined. I sat on a chair while the nurse burned the warts off one of them. In another bed, a doctor was doing a biopsy; I waited.

"You have to use condoms with your *Pepes*[52], girl," I heard the nurse saying casually to the youngest woman.

"Some of them refuse and others are in hurry and don't even bother to look for it."

"One of these days you're going to catch gonorrhea or *SIDA*[53], and you will die."

"It's not easy! It's not easy, darling."

---

51. "He cheated on you."
52. Foreign clients of prostitution, "Johnnies."
53. The common way to referred to HIV.

Wasn't prostitution abolished in 1959? What were they talking about?

"Another one with *condiloma!*" the nurse yielded after examining me.

"Honey, your case is so clear that we don't need any further exams. You have to come for treatment every week. Warn your partners and your partners' partners," she said.

I confronted Anselmo.

"All these years, we have shared the same ideals, the same bed, and our three children. From now on, we will share our ideals and our three children, but not the bed anymore." I told him firmly.

Anselmo took his belongings to the Calixto García where he worked at the time, but the hospital was already overbooked with other separated and divorced doctors who were practically living there; there wasn't any space left. Soon, Anselmo's back started hurting from sleeping on top of two chairs.

"You can sleep in my bed if you don't dare to touch me," I said happy to learn that he wanted to keep sleeping in our bed. I always preferred to sleep with company. I had panic of the night and all those years that I shared a bed with Anselmo I felt secure and slept soundly through the night. When he wasn't home, I had nightmares and I woke up in the middle of the night sweating and afraid of wetting my bed again. Some nights I even kept a kitchen knife under my pillow, not to harm anybody but to kill myself if the panic became too intolerable.

Anselmo had been a great father and husband. He went through a bad phase five or six years before the diagnosis of my *condiloma*. He developed a kind of illness that pushed him to seek other women like a maniac. He kept saying that he loved me and made love to me, but next day he was seeing someone else, and next week someone different.

We separated, but nothing changed much, anyway. Many nights we slept in the same bed. Anselmo kept bringing his salary home, and he was still registered in our household to get his foodstuff. Where else could he go? Life just went by the same way it had gone by before. Isa, Pedrito, and Boris were already grown and our separation didn't affect them much; they'd never spent much time with Anselmo, anyway. They kept busy with their own lives—Isa studying psychology, Pedrito starting his degree in chemistry, and Boris filling out the forms to study journalism. The three of them also volunteered with the *Contingentes obreros,* constructing houses, roads, clinics, and childcare centers. Isa would live years later with her new husband and their son Tonito in one of those *microbrigadas* she helped build along with her brothers in Alamar.

It wasn't our separation that changed the course of our life but a silly inoffensive old book about animals that Isa read to Camila at night; a tale about pigs and horses, dogs and hens, chickens and goats. My children gossiped about that book and lowered their voices retelling the tale. "It's been very hard to get it! There are only a few copies in Havana," I'd heard Pedrito saying. The book wasn't prohibited, it was simply not allowed. I had the same panic I felt many years ago when I heard one of my children singing out loud the song by the Beatles that went "let it be, let it be, let it be, let it be" or another one that went like "Yesterday, all my troubles seemed so far away. Oh yesterday came suddenly."

It wasn't like the police came arresting whoever sang those songs or read certain books, but the Beatles, as were many other groups and singers, and many writers, were considered harmful. If I discovered a tape of the Beatles in my house, I would throw it away scolding my children and accusing them of *diversionismo ideológico*[54], as I was told I should do. *El Comandante* himself had

---

54. Ideological deviation, or "ideological diversionism." The terms refers to civil behavior that showed lack of "true revolutionary commitment." Raul Castro often used the term as a moral reprimand referring to the

accused the Beatles of being subversive, imperialist, and symbols of a selfish consumerism.

I shouldn't have read that dammed book about animals, but I did.

"Liberty! Liberty! Liberty!" the Animals of the Manor Farm demanded after listening to the brilliant speech of a charismatic pig named Major. "Man is the enemy of animals and we must rebel against him," the pig said.

"In fighting against Man, we will not resemble him. Even when we conquer him, we will not adopt his vices. No animal must ever live in a house, or sleep in a bed, or wear clothes, or drink alcohol, or smoke tobacco, or touch money, or engage in trade. And, above all, no animal must ever tyrannize over his own kind. No animal must ever kill any other animal. All animals are equal!" old pig Major concluded.

"We are all equal!" the animals of the Manor Farm shouted in frenzy,

The Rebellion of the animals was successfully carried out, Man was expelled, and the farm took the new name of Animal Farm.

"Whatever goes upon four legs, or has wings, is a friend; whatever goes upon two legs is an enemy!" the animals yelled in the wildest excitement destroying everything that reminded them of Man: the whips, the reins, the halters, the blinkers, the degrading nosebags, even the ribbons with which the horses had been decorated on market days. The farm was theirs! The leaders of the Rebellion took the animals to the store-shed and served out a double ration of food. After that, the animals settled down for the night and slept as they had never slept before. The animals were happier than they had ever conceived it possible to be. Every mouthful of food was an acute pleasure, now that it

---

"diversionist" as an example of all the bourgeoisie vices, habits and values.

was truly their own food, produced by themselves, not doled out to them by a gradging master.

The work of teaching and organizing Animal Farm fell upon the three cleverest pigs, Snowball, Napoleon, and Squealer who had elaborated old Major's teaching into a complete system of thought called Animalism. Once the other animals accepted the pigs as their teachers, they absorbed everything they said.

"Comrades, now we need to fight against Man's past mistakes," Squealer, a brilliant talker, said, "Your beliefs were based on Man's beliefs and they are wrong!" Although the animals did not understand Squealer's long words, his explanations were very persuasive and his arguments taken as the ultimate truth.

The animals were busy organizing themselves in Animal Farm. Napoleon took over the education of young puppies that were taken away from their mothers as soon as they were weaned. Snowball got especially busy organizing the Animal Committees. He formed the Egg Production Committee for the hens, the Clean Tails League for the cows, the Wild Comrades' Re-education Committee with the object to tame the rats and rabbits, the Whiter Wool Movement for the sheep, and various others, besides instituting classes in reading and writing that were a great success; soon almost every animal was literate in some degree. The pigs could already read and write perfectly. The dogs learned to read fairly well, but were not interested in reading anything except the New Commandments of Animalism that were summarized in "Four legs good, two legs bad!"

The food was distributed in an equal manner, until the day some animals found that the pigs were receiving a greater ration of milk and a larger portion of apples than the rest.

"Comrades!" cried Squealer, "The whole management and organization of this farm depends on us and it's for your sake that we drink that milk and eat those apples. If we pigs fail in our duty, Man could come back to Animal Farm; absolutely no animal wanted Man to come back to the farm.

The pigs had prohibited the animals to have contact with the world outside Animal Farm because although human beings had been defeated, they might make another attempt to recapture the farm and reinstate Man. The new foundation of Animal Farm demanded loyalty and obedience.

"We need discipline, comrades, iron discipline!" Napoleon said.

Through the years, the animals worked as slaves. Sometimes difficulties came from inside the farm, some other times it was the weather, too much rain and a flood, or too little rain and a draught, a terrible wind. Often, the food fell short and the corn rations were drastically reduced. For days at a time the animals had nothing to eat; starvation seemed to stare them in the face. There were voices of discontent, but were promptly silenced by a tremendous growling of dogs, and the sheep would break into "Four legs good, two legs bad!" and the momentary awkwardness was smoothed over.

"There is no food shortage on Animal Farm!" Napoleon claimed, and as an emergency measure, he decreed that the hens must surrender their eggs to be sold to farms that would pay to keep Animal Farm working. The hens had been warned that this sacrifice might come, but had not believed that it would really happen. They were just getting their clutches ready for the spring sitting, and they protested that taking the eggs away was murder. For the first time since the expulsion of Man, there was something resembling a rebellion against the Rebellion. Many animals were executed at that time, confessing crimes they didn't commit, but Napoleon used clever techniques that convinced even the most upright animals to confess to cruel crimes.

Life was hard, winters cold, and rations short. A few animals still remembered the old days of the Rebellion and the dreams and enthusiasm they felt about having a farm where animals were free from hunger and the whip. Instead, they were starving to death, no one dared speak his mind, and comrades were torn to pieces after confessing to shocking crimes. According to the pigs, though, the improvement had been enormous and Napoleon constantly read figures proving that nowadays the animals had more oats, turnips, and hay; they had more straw in their stalls and suffered less from fleas than in the days of Man. The water was also of better quality. Animals worked shorter hours, lived longer, and a larger proportion of their young ones had survived infancy. The animals were glad to believe Napoleon's words. Besides, many of them didn't remember the old days anymore.

"Long live Comrade Napoleon!" They all shouted. The youngest recited poems composed in Napoleon's honor while the pigs gave speeches about the latest increases in production of foodstuffs. Whatever happened, the animals remained faithful, worked hard, carried out the orders given to them, and accepted the leadership of the pigs. The animals saw no reason to disbelieve the pigs, especially as they could no longer remember very clearly what conditions had been like before the Rebellion.

Years passed, many of the leaders of the Rebellion died, and the Rebellion became a mere tradition passed on by word of mouth. It seemed that the farm had grown richer without making the animals themselves any richer, except for the pigs and the dogs, but still neither pigs nor dogs produced any food by their own labor. For the other animals, life was as it had always been; they were generally hungry and worked tirelessly in the fields; in the winter, they were troubled by the cold, and in the summer by the flies. The older animals tried to dig into their memories to see if things had been better or worse before the Rebellion, but they couldn't remember; they had to trust the lists of figures with which the pigs demonstrated that life was getting better and better.

The animals never gave up hope and never lost their sense of honor, dignity, and privilege in being members of the only farm owned and operated by animals. If they went hungry, it was not *from feeding tyrannical human beings; if they worked hard, at least they worked for themselves. No creature called any other creature 'Master' and all animals were equal.*

Until the day when a horrifying vision struck Animal Farm and turned the lives of all animals, once again, upside down.

"It's Squealer walking on his hind legs!" cried out a goat.

It couldn't be! But after Squealer, came a long line of pigs walking on their hind legs. Some kept a perfect balance better than others. After the long line of pigs surrounded by protective loyal dogs, came Napoleon himself walking majestically upright. Napoleon was carrying a whip on his trotter. There was a deadly silence. Amazed, terrified, and yet in shock the animals watched the spectacle of the pigs walking on two legs. Some animals were ready to protest when the sheep burst out into a tremendous bleating of "Four legs good, two legs better! Four legs good, two legs better!" By the time the sheep had quieted down, the chance to protest had passed.

The New Commandments of the Rebellion had been rewritten on a wall, now summarized as:

All animals are equal

but some animals are more equal than others.

After that scene, the animals were not surprised to see the pigs wearing Man's cloths, smoking Man's cigars, sleeping in Man's bed, and eating at the table with Man himself. Pig and Man had come to terms. It was a source of great satisfaction to Man and pig that a long period of mistrust and misunderstanding had come to an end. The pigs invited Man to visit the farm and Man was content to see that Animal Farm was run with a discipline and an orderliness which should be an example to all farmers everywhere, and that the lower animals on Animal Farm did more work and received less food than any animals in the surrounding area.

Outside, the frightened animals were looking through the window. The oldest ones witnessed how yesterday had come suddenly to Animal Farm.

Man and the pigs were giving toasts with glasses full of beer, "For the prosperity of the Manor Farm! Long live Manor Farm!"[55]

How in the hell could anybody in 1945 write a story in an English village that reflected our lives in Cuba half a century later?

---

[55]. Words taken from Rosa's own recalls and stored memories, and completed with excerpt from the allegorical and dystopian novel by George Orwell published in England, 17 August 1945.

Chapter 10
AVE, FIDEL! CUBANS MORITURI TE SALUTANT[56]

I turned fifty the same year that we celebrated the thirty-first anniversary of Fidel's victory over Batista, and the same year that started the disintegration of the Soviet communist bloc. That was 1990, when the Soviet Perestroika and the *Bloqueo* of the United States conspired together against the Island provoking the worst crisis in Cuban history.

As I was turning fifty, the socialist bloc was abandoning us, and *El Norte* was taking advantage of our isolation to screw us more. We would need to sacrifice our lives more defending the Revolution, *¡Socialismo o muerte!*

Until that moment, I hadn't realized how much we had all depended on the Soviets' will to protect and provide for us. We had lived all those years without really thinking what would happen if the Soviets stopped sending us their aid in food and supplies.

"*El Norte* wants us all dead. The *yanquis* will not stop until we sink," Mima said.

"Blame it on Russian communism, not los yanquis," Pedrito said.

"It's been neither los *yanquis* nor the Russians; it's been the mistakes of the Revolution; I heard it on the radio," said Boris in a low voice.

---

56. Original quote in Latin: *"Ave, Imperator, morituri te salutant"* or *"Ave, Cæsar, morituri te salutant"* "Those who are about to die salute you."

"What are you talking about, son?" Anselmo asked.

"I didn't tell you before because I knew you would be mad at me. *Radio Martí* is broadcasting from *El Norte* and I've been listening to it for a while at my friend Yarik's house.

"Are you crazy, Boris? Do you want to end up in prison?" I asked.

"You see? That's exactly why I haven't told you before," he said.

Beginning with that day, Boris irritated us with stories he heard on *Radio Martí,* which reminded me of Amalita's antirevolutionary criticism. One day he came saying that Fidel had five luxurious houses in Europe while our houses in Havana were falling apart; another day that Fidel had bought machines from the Russians to cut the cane but the *bolos*[57] had fooled him sending snow plows instead; another day that Fidel had cut the plantain trees to harvest coffee and that all the coffee plants had died and we Cubans would have neither plantains nor coffee for decades. Another story was that Fidel had failed in his cow milking experiments, "That's why our rations of milk have decreased, Mami."

Whatever the reason, the U.S. blockade, Russian *Perestroika*, or the Cuban Revolution itself, or the three together, the fact was that Amalita's prediction was right, the Island was sinking and we were all sinking with it.

When November came, *El Comandante* stated that Cuba had lost the economic assistance from the Soviet Union and the socialist countries and we were entering a new phase, the "Special period in time of peace," *Período Especial* we called it. Cuba would be immersed in a deep economic crisis that would affect all sectors of society with potential consequences for our survival as serious as those of a war. It was hard to believe since we didn't feel these consequences immediately. I didn't take it seriously.

---

57. Derogatory term to refer to Russians.

"It's never been easy here, anyway. We'll deal with it! It can't be as bad," I thought.

For the first time since 1972, Katinka disagreed with me, "It's very bad and we'll die," she announced.

At the end of 1991, Year Thirty-Three of the Revolution, Robertico Robaina, the Minister of Exterior Relations, said "we are ready to distribute the same nothing in equal parts." We then knew it was the end. The plan this time was called *Opción Cero*, Zero Option—zero energy, zero electricity, zero transportation, and zero resources.

The Russians kept promising their unconditional aid, but when the shipment from the *CAME* didn't come on time, we realized we were sentenced to die. Without food, without gas, without electricity, and without water life became the worst nightmare imaginable. Mima and I spent more time than ever trying to invent something to eat at least once a day. It broke my heart to see Camila going hungry.

"*Abuela,* what about if we eat paper?" she said one day. But there wasn't much paper to eat anyway.

Many days we began our morning with *agua con azúcar,* water and sugar, and went to bed with water and sugar. Whenever I could, I boiled a little rice, without salt and without oil, and almost without either water or rice and gave it to Camila, then to Mima, and then to my children, "Go ahead and finish it all, I'm not really hungry," I said.

I lost sixty pounds in a few months. I walked like a zombie, as did many others; we were all so undernourished and weak that nobody felt like walking, or talking, much less smiling. We stayed at home. There were no cars on the roads. One could lie down on the road of *Calle 23,* the once really busy 23rd Street, for hours without any fear of being run over a car.

It was not easy! For years and years the state had given us everything, so we didn't need to develop strategies for survival. We had lived protected by the state until then. After the 1990s we were on our own and in order to survive we needed to invent; we all became inventors in one way or another; it was not easy!

"Mami, today I ate a *bocadito de frazada.*"[58] Boris said one day, "it filled me up."

Pedrito and Boris had been experimenting making sandwiches with different kinds of rags that they boiled in the express cooker, "we found a rag that doesn't taste as bad as the others and the chewing is easier; you should try it," Boris said.

They also made "steaks" of grapefruit peel fried in mineral oil, "cheese pizza" with melted condoms from China, "beef burgers" made of green banana peel, "fruit juice" made with urine and mashed orange peel. However, the *bocadito de frazada* and the shake of yam became Boris and Pedrito favorite. The rest of us ate a little bit of white rice one day, a piece of bread with green fungus two days later, one boiled egg divided into parts for several of us. Cabbage was basically the only thing we could eat more or less regularly, but sometimes not even that. I learned to prepare so many different dishes with that damned cabbage.

"What are we going to eat today?" became my morning question, "what are we going to eat tomorrow?" was my nightly one. How to get food to feed my family became an obsession that I couldn't control. The less food we had, the more I thought about eating.

But it wasn't only food we needed. We had no soap or detergent to wash our clothes and we had to turn to salt and water. Our farms didn't receive the agricultural chemicals they needed for the food production like herbicides, fertilizers, fuel for the machinery, and irrigation pumps. We had no construction materials either; no hospital equipments. Many factories closed for lack of materials. The lack of gas, oil, batteries, and tires crippled the old busses, trucks and cars. People started using

---

58. Rag Sandwich

heavy weight Chinese bicycles instead of automobiles. Electricity blackouts left the Island in the dark. Stores, offices, and homes darkened as electrical shortages became more regular.

"*Ave,* Fidel," Boris shouted when *El Comandante* was on TV talking about the progress of the Cuban socialism:

"We will never give up socialism, because without socialism and without the Revolution we are nothing. Without the Revolution, we would have to return to the horrendous capitalist past that we all know so well. In spite of the blockade and the difficulties, our Revolution can proudly say that in this country there are no children without school, no sick person without a hospital, and that our infant mortality rate is under 10, much lower than in the so called developed countries."

"Cubans *Morituri te salutant,*" Pedrito concluded Fidel's speech with sarcasm, "Why doesn't he say that schools suck and that the level of teachers' absenteeism is comparable to or higher than before the Revolution? Why doesn't he say that teachers are forced to change the grade of the students to keep up the high standards? Why he doesn't say that pregnant women at risk are forced to have an abortion to avoid after birth complications that could increase the infant mortality rate?"

"Numbers! Numbers!" Isa followed, "All that matters is to maintain the numbers so the rest of the world admires the stoicism and sacrifices of the Cuban people."

"Long live Animal Farm!" Boris shouted.

It was good we didn't have much to cook because we had no matches to start the stove either. We left the stove on for days because we feared that if we turned it off we wouldn't be able to start it again in case we needed it; that was dangerous, we knew, but what could we do? A family died in Havana because they went to sleep leaving the stove on, then the gas was cut and the flame went out. When the gas returned in the middle of the night, it killed the whole family while they were asleep. The lack of alcohol and *luz brillante* meant that many families had to steal wood and cook in prehistoric times making fire in their own homes, exposing themselves to hazards that could cost their lives.

I was fortunate to be menopausal at that time and didn't have to worry about my period because the lack of sanitary napkins became a nightmare for women and girls who were forced to use pads made of worn-out bed sheets and towels. We were right back to the times we lived at the *solar* when I had to wash our cloth pads and hang them outside to dry in the full view of all the neighbors.

At least, when the blackouts were scheduled and announced, we prepared ourselves ahead of time to watch the *telenovela*. When it was our turn for the blackout, we all went to Kati's house whose neighborhood *apagones*[59] had been scheduled for different days of the week than ours. On the days of Kati's blackouts, she would come with her family to our house so they didn't miss any of the episodes of *Vale todo*[60] that drove us all crazy. In the evening, there wasn't a single soul in the streets of Havana, everybody was watching Raquel straggling to recuperate her daughter María de Fátima who was capricious, selfish, and capable of doing whatever it took to satisfy her own ambitions and to achieve her dream of becoming rich and powerful. She even sold her family's house to seek a glamorous modeling career in Rio de Janeiro, leaving her poor mother Raquel homeless and penniless, all alone in the world.

"Fátima is going too far," my neighbor Elvira said.

"She is such a vicious and unscrupulous woman," Angelina followed.

---

59. The *apagones* or electric blackouts were endured by Cubans almost everday during extended periods, during the 1990's economic crisis known as "The Special Period in Times of Peace".
60. "Everything is Valued."

"It is normal that Fátima is ambitious and selfish. Raquel never had sufficient time to spend with her daughter and the girl grew up wild and unsupervised," I suggested.

"But that has nothing to do with immorality," Mima said, "That girl is all mixed up, she is so immoral that she wouldn't blink to kill her own mother to get what she wants."

Raquel had spent most part of her life with her father in a small village outside Rio de Janeiro and had to work very hard to raise her daughter. No wonder she couldn't find the time to spend with her child.

"It's Raquel's own feelings of shame and guilt towards her daughter that makes things more difficult," Isabelita's psychological interpretation came out, "Raquel feels a compassion for her daughter that doesn't let her see Fátima as the cruel and selfish girl she really is."

"Vyery gwood, Isabel!" Kati agreed.

Raquel finally decided to travel to Rio and find her daughter. Poor Raquel, nothing compared to her suffering and struggle, not even our predicament. In Rio, she survived as an itinerant food vendor and with her strong will and intelligence eventually made it big opening a chain of small restaurants that she named *paladar*. If Raquel was capable of surviving all her difficulties, why couldn't we? Was Raquel telling us that eventually we would be able to beat the odds and win the battle against hunger and underdevelopment? While María de Fátima used trickery and deception to get ahead, her modest mother Raquel refused to compromise her integrity. We Cubans were Raquel, the rest of the world was María de Fátima.

When the blackouts came unexpected, we would take Boris' radio that used batteries and listen to the news or music until the batteries ran out; we would sometimes have to wait months to be able to get more batteries.

Sometimes Boris took the radio outside to the balcony and raised the volume so everybody could hear *Radio Exterior de España* or *Radio Martí*. Other times he sang on the balcony "*Ya vienen los apagones, no me toques los cojones.*"[61] And next day we would have to apologize to the neighbors or to the president of the CDR.

"Boris is a good boy, you know that. We'll take care of him; don't make a big deal out of this," I insisted to the president.

"You can't let him talk like that, Rosi. If he keeps misbehaving, we'll have no choice other than report him and he will have to spend time in rehabilitation."

One day, I went to the bathroom and I saw on the floor, ripped apart, the pages of the Manual of Konstantinov.[62]

"What is going on, Boris?" I asked

"Mami, haven't you heard that Communism is dead? We don't need these books anymore. Instead of wiping our butts with the old reports you bring from the Ministry, we could do it with <u>Granma</u> or with Konstantinov, don't you think?

"How dare you say that? You're going to give us a heart attack, Boris. Don't you see that we need to make Communism stronger?"

"I don't understand why you are so blind, Mami."

"You should be grateful to Fidel and the Revolution!"

"For what?"

"For what you are! Do I have to remind you that your grandparents were poor and barely know how to read and write?"

---

61. A rhythmic Cuban jingle, "The blackouts are coming, don't dare to touch my balls."
62. The original name of the book was *Manual de economía política* by Konstantinov et al, edited by the Soviet Academy of Science. The book was an obligatory text at the University of Havana, used to set some of the foundations of the Marxist-Leninist Phylosophy.

"Life changes and countries evolve with time, so do people. We don't need the Revolution to teach people how to read or write. Have you even thought that without the Revolution we would have been much better off?

"You don't understand because you didn't have to live during Batista's time."

"Unfortunately no; unfortunately I had to live in my own time in this shit and be miserable. Look at me and tell me what I have that is different from what you had before the Revolution."

"I see opportunities for you that I've never had."

"I see nothing, just nothing. I don't have a *kilo*[63] in my pocket, I have nowhere to go for fun, I can't have a girlfriend because there is no place to go, my stomach is empty, I can count my ribs, and I'm not even allowed to speak up for fear of being imprisoned."

With no light at night, no candles, and no fan to ease the summer heat, I sat on the rocking chair with Camila on my lap, doing nothing, passing time and hoping it would pass fast, really fast. Was I the goat of Animal Farm as Boris had suggested? Was I the hen giving up its eggs? Was I the loyal dog growling to defend the undefendable?

"Will you prepare a nice *Quince* birthday party for me, *abuela*," Camila asked me after having hot water and brown sugar for dinner, *sopa de gallo* we called that brew.

"I don't know, *mi'ja*. What makes you think about your *Quince* party now? It's too hot to think about celebrations, and besides, you still have many more years to go. Who knows what will happen when you turn fifteen."

"How was your *Quince* party?"

"That was the happiest time of my life, but not really because I turned fifteen but because I had just stopped wetting my bed."

---

63. One *kilo* refers to one cent of a Cuban peso.

"How come?"

"I stopped urinating in bed a few days before I turned fifteen and my celebration was more about that than about my birthday. For my party, Mima borrowed some dresses from the miss she was working for as a maid, *señora* Mendieta, so we wouldn't have to spend *pesos* renting them. One of them was a red and white Spanish flamenco dress, and another a Charleston dancing dress. For the photo session we went to a studio, but we also took pictures at the *señora*'s house in Miramar. The studio pictures turned out beautifully, seven pictures in total with me all dressed and made up. I definitely looked older than fifteen. For one of the photos, I wore a bathing suit and sunglasses and I laid down like I was at the swimming pool although I hadn't seen a pool in my whole life. For days and days I slept with those pictures under my pillow. We didn't celebrate the party at the *solar*, but *señora* Mendieta prepared a really nice *merienda* for all of us and for her own children in their beautiful house, one of the most incredible houses I've ever seen. The entrance had big Spanish doors opening on to the courtyard, all surrounded be a tall black iron fence. They had a porch supported by white marble pillars. The courtyard was my favorite place. Their backyard was full of fruit trees: a mango tree, a lemon tree, an avocado tree, and they even had green grass that a gardener cut carefully with a big pair of shears. The interior of the house was incredible, so spacious, full of treasures: silver decorations, pictures on the wall, hundreds of pieces of glass, a fine China cabinet, beautiful and elegant Spanish furniture, very expensive and luxurious stuff. Mima was one of their cleaning ladies. Back then, the wealthy people had workers to do the cooking and the cleaning and the gardening and all of that. *Señora* Mendieta had two cooks, one for main dishes and the other for desserts, a gardener, a babysitter, and two cleaning ladies, one of who was Mima. My sister Mayda and I had lots of fun in that house. One time the Mendieta family left the country on vacation, and the four of us stayed there until they returned. Pipo watered the plants in the yard, and Mima kept cleaning the house as usual.

Meanwhile, Mayda and I would play at being wealthy and imitate the *gallego* accent from Spain "*once zapatos azul celeste.*"

Camila fell sleep, and as I cuddled with her on the sofa, I started wondering if I maybe urinated in bed for the fear I had of the night and of the Negro Man. *El Negro* was the beast of my childhood. "*Como venga el Negro les va a dar candela,*"[64] Pipo and Mima said terrifying us. If we were mischievous, *el Negro* would come in the middle of the night to pull us hard by the feet out of bed. Nothing could defend you against *el Negro* —resisting, crying, biting, screaming— he would take us no matter what.

That night I dreamed of Mima delivering washed and ironed clothes at a convent of Catholic nuns in El Vedado. "Girls! Stop running up and down the hallway," Mima said in my dream, "*Como venga el Negro les va a dar candela.*" Then a gigantic black man dressed with a long white gown approached us. The white veil that covered his head allowed me to see a cynical smile and a malevolent expression in his eyes. The black man started running after me. Mayda was gone; I could hear her laugh up above me as I was running for my life. The wicked black man dressed in a white gown was close to getting me when I woke up.

We lost weight, we lost our minds, we lost moral values, we lost hope, and we lost trust. We lost what we had achieved with the Revolution, and we were hungry, really, really hungry. Suicide became the only liberation for many who couldn't cope with the hardship, the sadness, and the deprivation.

One could pass close to neighbors or friends or relatives without recognizing them. Fat people turn into skinny, and skinny into skeletons. Young people got older in months, and old people died before it was their time to go.

The only member of my family who had an easier time was Isabelita, but only because she left the Island at the beginning of

---

64. "If the Black guy comes, he's gonna set you on fire."

1991 when the crisis was not so profound yet and we could still eat something.

At the beginning of the *Período Especial*, Isa was working as a clinical psychologist at the hospital *Hermanos Ameijeiras*. She was twenty-five and still single when she got the news that she had been accepted to do a two-year internship in a Madrid hospital.

"We have to help her go," Anselmo said, "Things aren't going well here, Rosi, and it would be better for Isa to be away for a while."

And so we did, we let her go, and it was good that the government didn't allow her to take Camila with her so she would at least have something important to return to us for.

"If you don't come back, I'll throw myself through a window," I swore to Isabel before she left, "and I'll take Camila with me!" I announced.

"I promise I will come back, I promise, Mami."

Isa left in July, and her first letter arrived three months later.

"I miss you all very much Mami, but I am very happy here. Life isn't easy, though. I have a hard time making decisions that seem easy for everybody else but me," she wrote in the letter.

One day, Isa would tell us later, she went with a friend to buy a blouse at *El Corte Inglés* and she felt dizzy from the moment she went in.

"It was like a jungle of things. I felt lost and disoriented," she said

"Do you need any help or are you just looking around?" the clerk asked.

"I need a blouse."

"What kind of blouse would you like, casual, formal?"

"I don't know. Are there more than one?"

"We have many more than one! We have hundreds! Look around. Do you see? Any color in mind?"

"A color in mind? What do you mean? Are there several colors?"

"We have many colors," the clerk didn't lose her patience but looked at Isa in disbelief. "Think about the color of your hair and your eyes and your skin and we can determine what color would be a good fit for you. I am going to give you some time to look around and I will come back a little later in case you need more help."

Isa couldn't make a decision; she was too overwhelmed. When the clerk showed up again Isa was not ready to make up her mind yet and her friend said to the clerk in a confident tone "She is from Cuba, you know?"

While Isa was having trouble making choices about a blouse or a pair of shoes, we were starving to death in the Island. Even with money, there was nothing to buy.

"There is no hunger in the Island! We have to make the Revolution stronger!" *El Comandante* said.

"We have to come out of this," I told my children. *"¡Patria o Muerte! ¡Venceremos!"* I used to say in the past. But, what about if, in fact, we died? *"¡Patria o Muerte!"* I whispered, and had no courage to end *"Venceremos."*

No time to die! Mima came out with her *guajira* soul and started inventing new recipes for the little food we had. Tired of "frying" eggs in water, she started frying pieces of chicken skin, used the left over fat to fry the eggs, and the little bits of chicken skin to prepare rice with "meat." She also made all kind of desserts with the same three ingredients: bread, water, and sugar.

"Today we have *Sorpresa de pan*!" She announced.

"First, we make a syrup with brown sugar and water," she instructed Camila, "Then we cut the bread in slices and put them in a frying pan. Pour the syrup over the slices of bread and fry it until tender. Do we have white sugar?"

"Yes, Mima, tons of white sugar."

"Then, we'll make caramel and pour it over the bread and we'll have our French toasts.

Another day, she made *Natillas de pan*.

"These hard pieces of bread can be used to kill an enemy, but we can mix the crumbs with white sugar and water. Do we have milk, Camila?"

"A little bit of powdered milk."

"Then instead of only water we can use some milk today. We boil the crams, the sugar, and the milk until we get a nice consistency and have 'Spanish custard'."

With Mima's recipes based on bread and sugar and sugar and bread, we gained some of our weight back. Although my one time lustrous butt looked more like a dry fig, and my boobs were just two pieces of skin hanging out over my body.

Chapter 11
ES-CUBA DIVING

We'd been holding on fine, until the day Camila couldn't walk to school. She got up from bed and fell down, tried to get up and fell down again crying.

"*Abuela*, I can't move my legs, I don't feel my legs!"

Pedrito was home, he put Camila on his shoulders and we all went to the *Calixto García* where Anselmo was on call. Mima came later with Boris.

"It seems that she has nerve damage in both legs but we are still analyzing her case," the doctor said after many agonizing hours of waiting, "She has to stay for observation and more tests."

"*Compañera!*" one nurse called me, "Bring some bed sheets for the girl, a towel, a light bulb, soap, and a warm dish to give her tonight."

"A warm dish? With what?" I asked, "With more sugar and water?"

"Don't worry, Mami, I'll get something for Camila tonight," Pedrito said.

They all went home and I stayed with Camila at the hospital. As he promised, Pedrito brought a dish for both Camila and myself, a kind of stew that Mima had cooked.

"Better don't ask me where I got the meat from," Pedrito said.

Camila's stomach had become so small that with two spoonfuls of the stew she was already full, "Don't cry *abuela*, I am going to be all right," she said trying to calm me down.

She was in the hospital for a month, just waiting to have some tests done. One day the X-rays machine didn't work, next day the machine worked but the technician wasn't there. More cases similar to Camila's started filling up the Calixto García and other hospitals until *el Comandate* spoke, "This is an epidemic sent by *el imperialismo yanqui*. The United States must be blamed!"

"To hell with imperialism, to hell with *El Norte*! I shouted, "When are they going to leave us alone?"

"We don't know what it is for sure yet, Rosi. Apparently is a neuropathy that in some cases like Camila's affects the lower part of the body. Lately we are getting more and more people with vision problems; people suddenly become blind," Anselmo said, "It is an epidemic of something we don't know about yet, but we have to find a cure or a way to prevent further infections."

Mima stayed with Camila during the day and I stayed at night. It wasn't easy to sleep all night on a chair. Sometimes when my old bones couldn't handle it anymore, I got in bed with her until we both fell asleep sharing tales and stories.

"Nurse! Nurse!" I called hysterically one night when I woke up and dared to turn the light on, "Nurse! Nurse! There are cockroaches everywhere!" I shouted while I tried to clean Camila's IV which was infested with dozens of little brown cockroaches crawling up and down the tube.

"Shut up, *compañera*!" the nurse said upset, "You're going to wake up the whole unit."

"What do you want me to do? My granddaughter is being eaten alive by these things."

"Why did you turn the light off?" she reprimanded me, "Don't you know that cockroaches come out in the dark? Leave the light on and they'll go away," she advised.

Close to Camila there was nine-year old Yaelis who was recovering from meningitis, and sixty five-year-old Georgina peacefully resting in the third bed after a stroke. The room looked like a carnival with the three bed sets of different colors: green, blue, and yellow.

"My *bisabuela* believes that babies are brought by a flying stork?" Camila told Yaelis one of those days when there was nothing to do but talk.

"How come?"

"I saw it with my own eyes," Mima defended herself, "When I was four, my little brother Joaquín was born and I swear I saw the stork flying out of the window of my *mamá*'s room;

"No way!" Yaelis said, "Babies come from their mother's bellies and through their vaginas."

"How do you explain then the big bloodstain on my *mamá*'s bed. Te beak of the stork must have hit her," Mima joked.

"Did you go to school and learn that?" Yaelis asked.

"I never learned that at school. I learned how to write and read, not very well though. I was the seventh of eleven children, some of whom went to school and some who didn't. My parents were *guajiros* and had to work very hard at the *central azucarero*, we called it *ingenio* back then, in the province of Matanzas. My big brothers helped my *papá* in the fields and my big sisters helped my mamá with the chores of the house; only the youngest could go to school, but the closest school was in a nearby town and we had to walk many miles everyday if we wanted to go. I couldn't finish Fifth grade because when I was ten, the central closed and we all had to move to a nearby town where my *papá* worked for a while as a carpenter and then as *hojalatero* buying and selling tin. My *papá*'s work was not enough to feed our big family and we were forced to split; some of my siblings stayed with my parents while my oldest sister Rosa Estrella, my brother Pedro, and I came to Havana to work."

"And what about you, Georgina?" Camila asked, "Did you go to school?"

"Of course I went to school!" Georgina sounded offended, "My parents weren't rich, but they made sure their nine children had a good education. My father was a house builder and my mother an elementary school teacher. All my siblings and I managed to go to the university, and in addition my father taught us all a craft. Besides being a historian, I became very handy working leather. Don't believe what people say nowadays that before the Revolution there were no options for women and that education was not a choice for the poor; that's not true. My parents made many sacrifices to send us to college, but that's the key, many parents weren't willing to sacrifice themselves for the education of their children because they didn't value education, but my parents did."

"Did you wear a blue scarf?" Camila changed the subject, bored of Georgina's speech.

"There were no children pioneers back then and I didn't have any blue scarf, not even a uniform."

"That was bad, you know," said Yaelis, "The blue scarf could have saved your life from an invasion of the United States."

"How come?" Georgina asked puzzled.

"I know, I know," Camila said raising her hand like in school, "You untie your scarf, you pee on it and put it fast over your mouth covering your face like this. You have to do it fast otherwise you die."

"Yes," said Yaelis mimicking the scene, "And you have to lie down on the floor after you pee on the scarf."

"I never learned that." Georgina said.

"Maybe you didn't go to school that day." Yaelis replied.

Glad of having an avid audience, Mima kept talking.

"Before I came to Havana, I'd never been in a big city and at the beginning I cried so much. I missed everything from the countryside, my parents, my siblings, the running around, the freedom. I missed sleeping in bed with my sisters; I missed the smell of my *mamá*'s cooking, the smell of the roasted coffee. I even missed the smell of the animals we had. The only thing I didn't miss was the *Ñáñigo* that probably was left behind somewhere in the countryside. The *Ñáñigo* was an old cruel black guy, a devil who grabbed children while they played, put them inside a sack, carried them far away into the hills, chopped their heads off, and sucked their blood. I never saw him, but I lived in terror of him. Other than that, our life was so simple and beautiful at the *central*. Life just went by helping my *mamá* and my sisters with the house chores: boiling sheets and tablecloths, sweeping the earth-packed floor, drying and roasting the coffee we grew at the back of our house. Boiling clothes stained with the dark dirt of Matanzas made life very difficult for our *mamá* who could easily spend four or five hours daily turning those black clothes into white shiny ones. The girls also helped washing vegetables and cleaning grains, peeling yucca, *malanga*, and sweet potato. My big sisters helped more with the cooking and the care of my *papá* and our big brothers; they had too much work at home. Every morning my *mamá* would go and put my *papá*'s socks on, and then his shoes, and even his shirt, and the old guy just jumped into his pants and left the house to work. In the evening when he came home, my *mamá* undressed him and gave him a bath before dinner. At the table, my *papá* also ate first, sometimes alone and sometimes with my big brothers, then the girls ate together. My *mamá* was the last one to eat, and when it was her turn, there was often not much left to eat and she would say 'I am not really hungry today,' and other times she said 'You eat it all, dear; I already ate,' or 'You go ahead and eat now, I'll eat later'."

"My *mamá* says that all the time," Yaelis interrupted, "Mothers are never hungry."

"My *mamá* was the first one getting up in the morning and the last one going to bed at night. The farm had neither electricity nor running water, and she had to cook in a wood-burning-stove for the thirteen members of my family. We had to work hard in the fields and around the house, but we also had time to play dolls. We made our own dolls with corncobs, the yellow silk of the corncob made a beautiful blond hair. My older sisters made corncob doll dresses with whatever piece of cloth or paper we had."

"My sister and I love playing with Barbies," said Yaelis, "My *papá* sent us four Barbie dolls from Miami, three of them are white and blond and the other one is a *mulatica* with bad hair like me."

"I didn't have much time to play dolls anyway, because before I turned 12, I started working as a maid with my sister Rosa Estrella in Havana. We became *internas* in a wealthy house in Miramar. A Catholic priest helped my sister to find a job where she could keep me close to her. My sister cleaned the house and I worked as the baby sitter for two little brothers, 2 and 4 years of age. Sometimes I had to help my sister with the cleaning but I spent most of my days caring for the little boys. Although Rosa Estrella and I shared a room in the house, many nights I had to sleep in the boys' room because they woke up in the middle of the night and their *mamá* asked me to care for them."

"My teacher told us that in Capitalism children had to clean bathrooms and beg in the street for food and my *mamá* says that maids were abused and that we're lucky now with the Revolution that gives good jobs to all. Fidel doesn't like women to be maids because that isn't a good job."

"I agree with Fidel, but at that time there were not many options for women," Mima turned her head towards Georgina, afraid of having opened a dialectical discussion. Fortunately Georgina had fallen sleep, and Mima kept talking:

"That was a good job for my sister and I because we could be together all day long and we didn't have to pay either rent or food. I worked in that house until I turned 15, when I met a young man and I left my sister to live with him; Ramón Tejedor was his name, a neighbor and friend of my brother Pedro who by that time had married and was expecting a child. Ramón was very charming and enchanted me from the very first moment I saw him at my brother's house. He was much older than I, and he knew how to treat a girl like me. We dated a little, not much, and we just took off and went to live together. My sister Rosa Estrella was very disappointed, she didn't approve of our relationship without being married; she wanted me to get married in the Church, but Ramón promised me to marry in the Church as soon as he could save enough money."

"What was the big deal?" Camila asked.

"My whole family was Catholic, Apostolic, and Roman, and we were all supposed to marry in the Church before living together. Money couldn't be the excuse because if we didn't have the money we should just date for years if necessary until we could save enough to get married in the Church. I felt really bad about that and I was very resentful of Ramón for not marrying me. But even before I got time to think much about my sinful situation, I was pregnant with my first child, your grandma Rosa, and a year later with my second, your aunt Mayda, and waiting, always waiting for Ramón to get enough money to marry."

Having Camila in the hospital was nerve breaking. The *Período Especial* affected all levels of our lives and the hospitals were no exception. We had to take our own sheets and wash them at home where I boiled them with a little bit of salt because we had no detergent. We also had to take our own light bulb. The hospital had no disinfectant to wash the floors or the toilets either. There was a lack of equipment, lack of medicines, lack of everything imaginable. The food was uneatable, even for the doctors who had to eat at the hospital. Doctors were weak and hungry. Surgeons had to perform life-threatening surgeries with only a banana in their stomachs for the whole day. Some doctors came to work from far away walking for hours or biking their heavy Chinese bikes; they arrived at the hospital exhausted and even disoriented. Some doctors decided to stay at the hospital overnight to avoid the long daily journeys, but there were no beds to sleep in and they had to sleep on dirty floors that hadn't been washed for weeks, with the lights on of course.

Back in the 70's doctors made many mistakes because they lacked the proper training with all the new Soviet materials. Once a man died in surgery because the anesthesiologist didn't know how to administer the Russian anesthesia. In the 90s doctors made mistakes because of their exhaustion, hunger, and lack of equipment. Doctors had to perform miracles with the few means they had.

In spite of all the challenges in the hospitals, patients didn't die massively as one could have expected; we Cubans have been made as strong as the devil's skin. Many deaths occurred nevertheless, and were not reported for fear that a higher numbers would spoil our proud medical record. One day a man was dying in a hospital in one district of Havana, he would be transported to another district that didn't have that many deaths that month. The same happened with expecting mothers at risk; the mother would be transported to a hospital with few infant deaths that month. Sometimes hospitals didn't want to accept a very sick person if the number of deaths had been greater than expected that month and the patient had to be shuttled from one hospital to another.

When Camila's neuropathy was finally diagnosed as *polineuritis periférica*[65], Anselmo said that the only way known to combat the symptoms was to give her high doses of vitamins, including folic acid, and all kinds of vitamin B. She was also prescribed a high protein diet which the hospital provided for two weeks: milk, chicken, and black beans; things that the rest of us hadn't eaten for a long time. I took Camila's leftovers home for Mima.

"You eat it, Rosi, you're working very hard and look tired and sick."

"No, Mima, you eat it, I'm not hungry."

---

65. Periferal nerve disorder. Condition that affected the periferal nervous system showing a wide spectrum of illnesses and a multitude of symptoms such as numbness, pain, burning or tingling, muscle weakness and sensitivity to touch.

Camila was released from the hospital, still unable to walk. Pedrito carried her everywhere, to the bathroom, to the street to play with other children, to the park, and to the hospital for more tests.

One day, the Vice Minister of Health, Terri was his name, was on TV talking with Fidel and publicly announced: *"Mi Comandante*, the *polineuritis* isn't caused by a virus but by malnourishment." A week later, he was removed from office and sent to *Oriente* to work who knows where. A new Vice Minister took his position.

"Why don't you go to the Catholic nuns for help?" Anselmo suggested, "I heard that they receive donations from Spain. Some of my patients go to Santovenia and the nuns treat them well."

"Are you kidding me? What do you want me to say when the nuns question me? That I am Catholic, Apostolic, Roman, and Marxist? Besides, Santovenia is a nursing home and not a center for donations."

"Then, maybe your sister can send us the vitamins from *El Norte*?"

"No way I'm going to implore Mayda. I won't beg her," I could hear Rolando's voice inside my head "You all got what you asked for. Why should we help you now?'

"*Hermana*," I said when the sister opened the front window of Santovenia, "My name is Rosi and I attended *Las Dominicas*, although I haven't practiced for many years," I said without breathing.

"You don't have to explain yourself, my daughter. Come inside and have something to drink."

"I'm Sor Antonia. What can we do for you?" she asked while serving me a cold Fanta.

"I haven't had a Fanta for thirty years, Sor, I might get a skin rash or something as a reaction," I joked, as I was nervous.

"What can I do for you?" she asked again.

"I heard that you help people in need."

"Currently, we help only the elderly. In the past, this convent served a large population; we did important charity work here in Havana. But that was in the 30's and 40's. After 1959, all the sisters left fearing to be burnt alive inside the convent, as communists had done with priests and nuns in Spain. But Fidel was reasonable with us, and many sisters came back when he assured us that we'd be fine and welcome as long as we only worked with people with mental disabilities and the elderly."

"My husband says that members of the Party are sending their elderly here. I wonder why here and not to the public nursing home?"

"Come and see, I'll show you around, and then you'll understand."

I walked around the convent, through the courtyard, inside the bedrooms, in the kitchen, even the toilets. The memories of *Las Dominicas* came so vividly to me that I felt vertigo and entered a state of hyper reality. I saw Mayda and my friends and Sor Francisca all signing "*es tu, Virgo Maria, a Domino Deo excelso, prae omnibus mulieribus super terram. Tu gloria Ierusalem, tu laetitia Israel, tu honorificentia populi nostri.*"

"*Alleluia, alleluia. Tota pulchra es, Maria et macula originalis non est in te...*" was coming from my mouth when the voice of Sor Antonia brought me back to the room where several elderly rested.

"This is José, he is eighty-six. Tell the lady why you like it here, José!" she commanded.

"I have eaten more chicken here in three months than in thirty years out there."

"The other nursing homes have no chapel, and I like to pray," said a lady in a wheel chair close to José.

"My house fell down on top of me while I was sleeping and two weeks later I woke up here surrounded by nuns dressed in white gowns; I thought I was dead and the nuns were angels," another man commented.

"I need a mother because mine can't take care of me," said a ninety-six-year old man crying, "Sor Antonia is my mother now."

"You see, my daughter? Our elderly here haven't experienced the *Período Especial*. Fidel gave us a prerogative to buy groceries at the stores. We also have a garden at the back of the house and the men and women who are capable, take care of it. As you know, private gardens are illicit in Havana but Fidel has given us this concession to help feed the 400 elderly we have. Taking care of the elderly helps the government a great deal, and in return the government gives us some privileges. Besides, now we are receiving donations in US dollars; nowadays without dollars it would be almost impossible to keep this house functioning."

"This is just a mirage, it's not real!" I said to myself remembering the words that I have heard hundreds of times during the past years, "Religion is only for the fanatics, it's just the product of a neo-colonial state in which the inhuman exploitation of the mass of workers brings misery and illiteracy, unemployment, ignorance, administrative corruption, prostitution, and a series of social maladies that in the past kept our country subjugated. It was only thanks to the Revolution that we could go through an anti-fanatic process that prohibited religion and opened us up to development and justice for all."

"It's not only food and care. We've offered the elderly the Catholic faith they professed when they were young. In their desire to keep living in the past, they have accepted the faith again; some of them believe they are back in their youth attending a Catholic school.

"No wonder!" I thought. I even had to restrain myself from kneeling down and confessing my sins!

"It's God's will! After many decades of Marxism, these elderly came here to die in the peace of God," Sor Antonia concluded.

At the end of a hallway I saw twenty or thirty elderly men standing up in a straight line. Behind a table there was a nun putting something inside a plastic basket.

"That is Sor Inés, she is collecting the dirty handkerchiefs; it's laundry day."

"The reason I came, Sor Antonia, is because my granddaughter has been diagnosed with *polineuritis periférica*. The government doesn't know for sure if this is a virus sent by *El Norte*, you know, but we heard that good nutrition and vitamins would help her get stronger and walk again. My ex-husband is a doctor but he can't get enough vitamins for the child, and the ration card is not very generous these days," I felt my face burning; there I was like my grandmother and my mother, begging to the Church.

"I'll see what we can do. I'll talk to the Superior Mother and in a couple of days we'll tell you what we can do, in the name of God."

With the multivitamins and the boxes of cereal fortified with iron that the nuns provided, Camila started walking again, slowly but steadily.

In 1993, Year Thirty-five of the Revolution, Isa came back as she had promised. Anselmo had been saving a little bit of gas for months to pick her up from the airport in his 1950 Chevrolet.

In my heart I wished Isa had stayed longer in Spain. Two years before I would have died if she told me that she was going to stay, but there I was wishing for my daughter not to come back to Cuba. I wanted to save her all the pain that she would feel after her arrival.

When Isa saw us at the airport, she said *"Pero caballero*[66], you all look like a painting of *El Greco*,[67] so pale and skinny. It seems that you've just come from a funeral."

She looked beautiful and gorgeously fat, as she had gained quite a few pounds. Some of those pounds would disappear soon though, when she took off all the layers and layers of cloths she had brought for presents and that made her sweat to death at the airport: two bras, several panties, three socks, two pairs of jeans, three shirts, two blouses, and on top of everything two jackets.

"What happened?" she asked on the way back from Rancho Boyeros, "I don't understand. Havana is deserted. There aren't even cats or dogs running around."

"The dogs have died, and people ate the cats," Pedrito answered before I could say anything.

"And is all the Revolution's fault," Boris added.

---

66. "Hey, man!"
67. "My goodness, man!"

Chapter 12
HAPPILY EVER BEFORE

Isabel stayed in bed for a month cursing the Revolution. I became frightened that the neighbors would hear and report her along with Boris and the rest of us.

"Am I losing my children?" I asked myself.

"Don't talk like that, Isabel," I scolded her the day she screamed "I shit on Marxism!"

"Don't forget that the Revolution has given you everything you have." The same rhetoric I had used with Pedrito before. What else could I say? "Don't forget that you are a psychologist because the Revolution educated you," I concluded anticipating Isa's response.

"Whatever the Revolution gave me it was not for free. I paid it off!" she screamed, "Six times! Six times I had to work in the fields with *la escuela al campo*[68]. I picked tomatoes, potatoes, coffee, guavas, and I even cut cane. Do you call this a free education?" she asked furiously. "Don't you see that everything we have done is a big lie? Don't you remember that in order to get what you call my free education, I had to lie and say that I had no relatives in *Estados Unidos* and that all members of my family had been agnostic or atheist for several generations? Don't you remember?" She yelled.

---

68. "School to Countryside Plan." Every school year, high school students and teachers are required to perform voluntary agricultural labor in the countryside. They stay in agricultural camps for several weeks as a part of a work-study project that has been one of the principles of the Cuban Revolution.

"The system isn't perfect, but it works and if we all worked together we can make it work better. Working in the fields was not paying off your education, Isa. That was part of your learning how to build a better society where all, children included, have to play their part."

"How much of my life do I have to give to the Revolution to be able to freely live my life?"

"You are missing the point, Isa. Your life is not just yours; we all depend on each other to make this work. Spain has made you more selfish. You shouldn't have gone in the first place."

"How can you say that? Spain has not made me more selfish, it has helped me realize that the Revolution has been just an experiment and we Cubans have been the laboratory rats. Of course my life is not mine here, it has never been."

"Lower your volume, Isabel. Somebody could hear you!"

"Listen! I am tired of living in silence. I want to scream that I got my period and that I have no *íntimas* to use this month unless a friend is kind enough to let me use her worn out pieces of towel. I want the whole world to know that communism sucks."

I could see that my children were growing further and further away from the ideals of the Revolution.

"What in the hell is this?" I asked going through the pages of several magazines I found under Boris's bed. *Tiempos Nuevos*, *Novedades de Moscú*, and *Sputnik*. Those magazines were so inflammatory against communism that my hands started shaking. *Tiempos Nuevos* said that the Cuban leaders had been living like millionaires while the rest of us Cubans had been asked to die of inanition defending the Revolution. *Novedades de Moscú* narrated horrible crimes that apparently Stalin had committed, and *Sputnik* talked about the violation of human rights during the government of Bresnev.

"They aren't mine, Mami, you should ask Pedrito," Boris defended himself.

"Sorry, Mami, it wasn't my intention to upset you, but it might be time for you to know the truth," Pedrito said when I asked him.

"I don't know what the three of you intend to do, but you are going to kill me with all of this. What truth are you talking about?"

"The truth about the Revolution, the truth about the trial and execution of general Ochoa, the truth about the escape of general del Pino, the truth about the involvement of Fidel with drugs, the truth about the lies of the government."

"What are you talking about?" I shouted, "Ochoa was found guilty of treason by the court, and del Pino was a dissident who escaped *pa'l Norte.*"

"Believe whatever you want to believe; that's your choice. But something that you could never deny is what we have lived in our own flesh. Boris and I could have been incarcerated for wearing the blue jeans that aunt Mayda brought us from *El Norte;* '*diversionismo ideológico,*' our professors called it, but the sons and daughters of the *pinchos*[69] could wear whatever they wanted. Some of our classmates wore fancy clothes, ate foods we'd never seen in Havana, drank imported alcohol, and had luxuries that were unthinkable for the rest of us. 'These aren't things from *El Norte,*' they defended themselves, 'My dad is a general and brought them to me from our friends the socialist countries.' I soon learned that in Cuba there were two classes of citizens, the ones who worked and produced and the parasites who lived without working or producing."

That phrase sounded familiar to me but I couldn't remember who said it or where I heard it before.

"It's Animal Farm, Mami, don't you see?"

Was life conspiring against me? Where did my little pioneers go? Where was that child Pedrito who wrote a poem dedicated to

---

69. Referring to the children of important Cubans, the children of the hierarchy, the children of the militars.

El Comandante and read it proudly in front of his class? Where was my sweet Boris who repeatedly say "I want to be like *el Ché*"? And what about my Isa who didn't want to wash her uniform because Fidel had touched it one day while visiting her school?

It was not only my children. The *Período Especial* hurt us tremendously, especially the youth. Hunger brought discontent, disenchantment, and desperation, and like Isabel, Pedrito, and Boris, the youth started complaining openly about everything, and for the first time also against Fidel. "Socialism is not the same with a full stomach as with an empty one," I heard Pedrito's friends saying.

"It is time to do something, Rosi," Anselmo said, "Otherwise we might have a revolution against the Revolution."

Anselmo was right! But what could we do?

The arrival of Elvirita's uncle to Santos Suárez took away the distress of those times and brought amazement, admiration, and the certainty that everything was possible in *El Norte*. The coffin with the mummified body of uncle Lalo departed from the international airport of Miami May 2nd and arrived in Havana two weeks later after having taken a trip through the Caribbean as uncle Lalo had stated in his will. Elvirita awaited the body of uncle Lalo with nervousness and expectation knowing that her cousin Ana had dressed the deceased with two pair of blue jeans--one Levis 501 and another Levis 505 for Elvirita's children, one pair of Nike shoes for her husband, several Calvin Klein shirts, layers of underwear, a pair or readers so grandma could keep sewing school uniforms, and dentures for grandpa so he could keep eating the *picadillo de soya*. Ana also promised to send all sort of groceries underneath the departed, between the wood and the silk lining.

When uncle Lalo finally arrived in Santos Suárez, Elvirita arranged a kind of memorial outside the apartment building because inside there was no place to accommodate the coffin. Several neighbors and relatives came to pay respect to uncle Lalo while Elvirita passed around a shake of sweet potato saying that it was made of pure mango. The wake went by with normalcy until a mischievous child dared to open the casket and loud music playing Beethoven's Ode to Joy came out from the box resonating throughout the neighborhood and beyond. Hundreds of children and grown ups came in procession from far away neighborhoods and lined up waiting their turn to open the musical box.

The magical sarcophagus of uncle Lalo was only a break from our national affairs. On 14th of July of the same year, 1994, Year Thirty-six of the Revolution, we heard on the news that a group of disaffected Cubans had stolen an old Second World War tugboat called *13 de Marzo* with the intention to flee Cuba and reach the coast of the United States. The boat left the port of Havana about 3:00 am. One hour later the tugboat was sunk, and 37 people drowned.

"The *13 de Marzo* sank simply because it was very old and not seaworthy," the authorities said that night on TV.

"This has been an irresponsible act of piracy promoted and stimulated by a counter-revolutionary radio station," *Granma* said in an article entitled "Capsized Tugboat robbed by Anti-Social Elements."

"This is what that dammed Radio Martí brings," I told my children angrily, "chaos, destruction, and death. This is what you want for our family? Look at the news!"

"Grandma is right!" Camila defended my position, "I heard at the school that Radio Martí is the weapon of *el imperialismo yanqui* and that all children of Cuba should rally against the enemy, defend our homeland, and defeat *imperialismo*."

"Like you know about imperialism and homeland!" Boris said upset.

"Why don't they leave us alone," Mima protested.

Two days later, *Granma* published a note from the Ministry of the Interior saying that the appropriate authorities had investigated the circumstances surrounding the sinking and found that it had taken place as a result of a collision between the *13 de Marzo* and another tugboat which was attempting to catch up with it. There had been like seventy something people involved in the escape, many of them members of the same family. The dissenters lived in five districts of Havana: El Cotorro, La Víbora, Marianao, Guanabacoa, and Arroyo Naranjo; nobody from Santos Suárez.

News and more news kept coming retelling the story of the incident, "The intercepted tugboat *13 de Marzo* did not stop on the order of the authorities, instead it continued to ward the open sea. Three tugboats did everything they could, but the *13 de Marzo* started sinking. Thirty seven people died and thirty one were rescued," said the TV.

A few days later, Pedrito and Boris came out with a very different story, which was hard to believe.

"The first tugboat that intercepted the *13 de Marzo* started to ram it in order to make it turn over," Pedrito said, "Another tugboat soon appeared and taking over from the first one continued doing the same thing. People were trapped between the two boats, which then began to direct water at them with high-pressure hoses. Many people were injured by the pressure of the water that threw them against the bulkheads of the boat."

"It was an unfortunate accident!" I said, "The tugboats were just doing their job. We all have gone through the same hardship but that doesn't mean that we are going to highjack a boat and leave the country. What these people have done is wrong; they were committing a crime."

"How can you say that, mother?" Boris continued. Calling me "mother" gave me an idea of his mood against me. "Do you forget that your own father left the Island? Was he committing a crime too?"

I decided for once to listen Radio Martí:

"The vessels that attacked the 13 de Marzo belonged to the Cuban Ministry of Transportation and are called "Polargo 2",

"Polargo 3" and "Polargo 5". According to survivors, "Polargo 5" was the vessel which acted most aggressively towards them. People screamed and implored the attackers to stop directing the water hoses at them because they might cause the children to drown. Instead of stopping, a third tugboat appeared and attacked the 13 de Marzo forcefully from behind, splitting the boat in two. People on board were submerged in the water. After nearly an hour of battling in the open sea, the other boats circled round the survivors, creating a whirlpool so that they would drown. As a result many disappeared into the sea and lost their lives. The tugboat that had split the stern went ahead and split the prow. There was no way to keep the tugboat afloat, it was sinking because the weight was all in the middle. The tugboats were not only responsible for sinking the 13 de Marzo but also for doing nothing and watching passively as the passengers drowned. When the boat started sinking, the other tugboats backed off but did not attempt to rescue the people on board. At no point did the pursuing vessels warn the passengers on board the 13 de Marzo of what they were going to do or give them any opportunity to give themselves up. On the contrary, the port authorities knew of the plot to hijack the tugboat. They then waited until the boat was far from shore so there wouldn't be any witnesses. They wanted to give a lesson to the disaffected, but the situation got out of hands."

I was stunned. "But the Cuban news said that those in the tugboats were civilians, ordinary dockworkers who were doing the right thing," I said.

"They were dressed in civilians' clothes but they were not civilians," Pedrito stated.

"The leader himself admitted to be irresponsible," I mentioned remembering the news again. "He deserved to be eaten by the sharks for taking not only men but also women and children in a boat that was built in 1879."

"Don't you see that the leader is still kept at *Villa Marista*[70] and is being pressured to change the story of what happened? Of course he admitted to be irresponsible, I would admit that I'm Napoleon Bonaparte if I were forced to do so."

"It's true, Mami. A colleague of mine who is a psychologist has been asked to go to *Villa Marista* and help force the prisoners to change their stories if necessary."

What a tragedy! The bodies were never recovered. Authorities claimed that it was not possible to locate either the victims or the sunken boat. Twelve children died, from ages 3 months to 17 years old.

In the days immediately following the tragedy, the authorities attempted to prevent any protest or public demonstration of grief. A mass for the victims was cancelled and relatives of the victims were prevented from throwing flowers into the sea.

"That is only done for 'martyrs of the Revolution' and the passengers of the *13 de Marzo* were dissidents, not martyrs," authorities said.

By the end of July there was no more news about the incident, but the tension kept building up, until one day, August 5th, less than a year after Isa came back from Spain, at around 2:30 in the afternoon, two friends of Pedrito came to the door looking for him. I wasn't home but Mima heard them saying "*Oye, esto se jodió! La gente está tirá pa' la calle gritando ¡Abajo Fidel!*"[71] Nothing Mima said could stop Pedrito from taking his Chinese bike and go to the *Malecón* to see what was going on.

People started by breaking bottles in the streets and making noise to express their discontent. Soon hundreds, and later thousands of Cubans were breaking the windows of state-owned

---

70. A very feared detention center in Havana, famous for the detention and the torture of political prisoners by the national security agency.
71. "Hey, this has fucked up! Everybody is outside in the streets shouting 'Down with Fidel'."

dollar stores near the *Malecón* and destroying tourist hotels while screaming "We are fed up! We want freedom! Down with Fidel!" They made barricades with garbage containers and took bricks and wooden frames from old buildings to use them as projectiles against the police that was trying to quell the demonstrators.

Pedrito arrived when almost everybody had been arrested but he saw people screaming

"¡Basta ya! ¡Basta ya! ¡Libertad, libertad! ¡Cuba sí, Fidel no! ¡Cuba sí, Fidel no!"[72] There were others counteracting those chants with louder voices *"¡Pin, pon fuera, abajo la gusanera! ¡Pin, pon fuera, abajo la gusanera! ¡Esta calle es de Fidel! ¡Esta calle es de Fidel!"*[73]

The revolt ended in a matter of minutes. We saw it all on TV that night. Fidel explained that the disturbances were caused by a subversive plan of the United States to provoke chaos, disorder, and discontent in the Island. "What kind of *libertad* are we talking about here?" he asked to the people, "The concept of freedom is understood differently everywhere, and we Cubans do not agree with the American concept of freedom."

El Comandante knew exactly how to ease our temper.

"Americans always talk about freedom," he said, "But in their own country there is more than one million abandoned children. Americans like to talk about freedom, but when George Washington declared their Independence, black slaves were not liberated. The United States exterminated the native Indians; the United States has made alliances with the most cruel dictators in Latin America, and has hired the most unscrupulous assassins to organize the counterrevolution in Nicaragua and here in Cuba; the United State, the world's freest country has paid criminals to

---

72. "Enough is enough! Enough is enough! Freedom. Freedom! Cuba yes, Fidel no!"
73. "To hell with the traitors! (*Pin pon*, out with the scum!). This street belongs to Fidel."

participate in this riot and to encourage subversion, sabotage, and terrorism in our homeland."

People applauded.

"What have we done to the United States that they hate us so much?" Mima was asking while the reporter closest to Fidel stated that hundreds of civilian supporters of the Revolution went to Malecón and ended the riot peacefully.

"That's not true!" Pedrito shouted upset; "I saw it with my own eyes. The paramilitary brigades were there hitting people. *El Contingente* Blas Roca was there too, those construction workers were not civilians defending the Revolution; they were trained killers dressing like civilians to end the revolt! I saw it, this time I saw it!" he kept saying.

Family members found themselves on opposite sides of the struggle, and the whole country was getting split along ideological lines. The discontent escalated to such a degree that people began daring to speak up and daring even to cross the sea on a raft to join the enemy of the North.

And it happened again, Fidel opened the gates and thousands of people abandoned their homes, their families, and the Revolution that brought them up. I thought about Mayda and Pipo, and about all of those people I loved who left, and I felt sick to my stomach.

"If one of you leaves the country, *me doy candela!*"[74] I told my three children, trying to prevent another rupture in my family.

"If I could, I'd leave," Isa said, "and I'd go to Madagascar."

"Is Madagascar in Spain?" Camila asked, "Would you take me there this time?"

"Don't worry, Mami, we are all too chicken to end up in Guantánamo," Pedrito said observing my panicked expression.

---

74. "I burn myself to death."

"Even if we want to leave, we wouldn't be able to afford it. Do you have any idea how much a raft costs?" Boris asked.

"How would I know? Why do you know?"

"*¡Radio Bemba!* People are paying 6,000 pesos for a raft, and 20,000 and 30,000 for a small boat. Not even working fifteen years could we save enough pesos to leave the country, so forget it! This time you don't need to burn yourself to death, maybe another time," Boris joked.

"I can leave if I want," Pedrito kept saying, "I don't need to buy a boat or a raft. I can use a door or whatever else that floats."

"Shut up! Please! You are all driving me crazy!" I said pulling my hair.

I don't know if it was loyalty to the Revolution, devotion to Cuba, family ties, or maybe fear of dying at sea, but despite my fears, none of my children left. I was lucky, because a month later Boris heard in the radio that more than 35,000 people had fled, most of whom ended up being caught and sent to Guantánamo.

Balseros, as we called the raftbuilders, worked for months in abandoned houses building their *balsas*: rafts, tires, inner tubes, doors, and makeshift vessels hastily cobbled together from anything found. Styrofoam was a frequently used material because it wasn't as difficult to find as other materials strictly controlled by the state. Because the investment was very high, in order to make the effort worthwhile *balsas* were often overcrowded. *Balseros* kissed their loved ones goodbye and left *pa'l Norte*. Some took their children with them, others left them behind.

The *Mariel*, the *Período Especial*, and the *Maleconazo*, overturned our lives. To ease the discontent of the population, the Ministry of Labor created new jobs that resembled private small business. If we paid taxes, we would be allowed to open a hair saloon in our bedroom, or a little restaurant in the dinning room, or a repair shop in the living room. That was the time when Mima started doing nails and fixing hair in the living room; illegal, of course, because we couldn't afford to pay fixed taxes every month when we didn't know if we were going to have clients. When Mima had *unos quince*, she fixed the hair and nails of girl who turned fifteen, and also of all her female relatives. That way, Mima earned a few pesos but she couldn't charge the neighbors very much as they were as broke as we were.

At the end of the year, the *Agro* was allowed again. The farmers could set prices by supply and demand, but their operations would be regulated and taxed by the state. The government announced that the opening of the markets was a necessity to save the Revolution, not a measure towards capitalism; officials had said the same in 1993 when the U.S. dollar was decriminalized again. Of course, most of us in the 90's didn't yet have access to U.S. dollars anyway. What a shame that twenty years earlier I had flushed down the toilet one thousand dollars that I found in the lamp! Still *El Comandante* had clearly said that it wasn't a permanent measure, that very soon the dollar would be illegal again, and that it was only a transition.

"When our economy recovers, the dollar will disappear!" he assured us. Since then, I have woken every morning thinking, "Will it be today when the dollar turns illegal again?"

In 1994, with the legalization of the U.S. dollar came also the creation of stores run by the government where we could buy products, most of them imported or donated from foreign countries. We called those stores *chopin* because the plastic bags for the merchandise said "easy shopping." Why in the hell was it written in English if only Cubans went there? Products sold at these stores were extremely expensive. In fact, the taxes were 240% on each product, which in theory helped to subsidize the stuff rationed by the state through our ration card.

Despite the high prices of the farmers' market and the *chopin*, we welcomed both as the only options to improve our lives.

It was then that I decided to rent and sell my illicit novels by Corín Tellado. In December, when the markets were also authorized for crafts and other products, Boris started selling piles of Soviet books and Cuban magazines we had kept in the house for decades; the Russian dictionary went first.

"Who in the hell would want to buy old editions of <u>Granma</u>, <u>Juventud Rebelde</u>, or <u>Bohemia</u> if everybody in Havana is sick of them?" Isa asked Boris.

"¡*Los yumas!*" he answered, "The city is now full of foreigners, tourists wanting to buy all these relics as souvenirs of a dying communism in the tropics."

Boris was right. *El Comandate* had no choice but to open the flood gates:

"We need foreign investment!" he announced, "It is a necessity to exploit our natural resources; it was not a necessity before. But now, we cannot rescind the natural resources of our country. We cannot leave our sun, our beaches, and our seas without being exploited."

With that openness came all the goods and evils that had been unknown since 1959. In 1993 alone, more than 500,000 foreigners, mostly from Canada, Mexico, Spain, and Italy visited our Island and become the main recipients of our wonders, including our young women and girls. Cuba wouldn't be the same anymore.

That was the time when a gentleman from Spain came to the neighborhood knocking door-to-door asking for Angelina Benitez Sarmiento.

"It's me!" Angelina said the day the gentleman knocked on her door, "How can I help you *compañero*"?

"Your husband, God have him in His Glory, inherited lands in Galicia from his parents and you're the only beneficiary; all other people with rights over that land have died."

"It can't be! My husband died twenty-five years ago. He never said anything about having lands in Spain."

"It has taken me years to find you. I have interests in that land and have come to make a deal with you. I can offer you $10,000 in cash. Think about it; I don't have much time. I'll come back in two days."

How could Angelina say no to such an offer, even if it wasn't true? In the middle of the *Período Especial* and only one year after the dollar had been legalized again! All of us longing for dollars and Angelina gets 10,000 without moving her butt from home; unbelievable!

All neighbors had something to say:

"Don't be stupid! Even if you aren't the person he is looking for, take the money. Who cares? This is no time to say no to an offer like this.

"If he came all the way from Spain to make the deal with you is because the land is worth much more than what he wants to pay you."

"Take the 10,000 and shut up!"

"Ask him for more!"

"Ask him to take you to Spain to see the land!"

"If you don't close the deal fast, he might return to Spain and you will not see either the land or the money."

Angelina took the $10,000 and became a national hero in the neighborhood, a living proof that miracles existed. She had never had so many friends and relatives in her whole life. Her popularity increased along with the envy and jealousy of those who longed for an inheritance from wherever around the planet.

In January of 1995, Year of the Centenary of the Fall of José Martí, the government introduced another currency, the *peso convertible*, with the same value as the dollar; we called it *chavitos* or *divisa*. The intention was to gradually establish the circulation of this currency to replace the U.S dollars, but that never happened and we had to struggle with the three currencies: *peso*, dollar, and *divisa*. One of the problems generated by the decriminalization of the dollar and the establishment of the *divisas* was that the Cuban *pesos* lost nearly all value because there was so little we could buy with them.

I said to myself "What is the point of keeping my job at the Ministry if I can't buy anything with my monthly salary of 250 *pesos*?" It wasn't worth it anymore. Every day, I spent four or five hours in transportation; I had to take a bus and a *camello*, one of those horrible buses with two humps like a camel that could fit 400 smashed together human beings. I left early in the morning and came back exhausted late at night, and with my salary we could barely survive the first two weeks of the month.

Our Social Security Law established that working women over fifty-five could retire after twenty-five years of work, so I did! I was lucky I could retire legally and get my 180 pesos every month. For people without twenty-five years of service, it was very hard to quit their jobs as anyone who abandoned a job became suspected of getting money illegally and could end up in jail. Work absenteeism was less suspicious than the abandonment of a job. That happened to my neighbor Elvirita, who at fifty-nine and with less than thirty years of service couldn't quit her job, but her absenteeism increased to the degree that at the end of the month she only received a symbolic salary of approximately 30 *pesos*. But Elvirita couldn't care less about her official job; her main income came from renting two rooms of her apartment to foreigners who paid $15 per night. When the business was good, she could easily get $900 in one month; an unthinkable amount of money for Cubans since a surgeon's salary was an average of $30 a month. Of course, Elvirita faced great risk for renting her bedrooms because she didn't declare it as a legal business and anyone in the neighborhood could denounce her to the authorities. She preferred to take the risk anyway since many months of the year she wouldn't be able to afford the fixed amount of $100 taxes. Besides, she trusted the good will of neighbors who had known her for decades.

"Who is going to denounce me?" she said convinced that all her years of commitment with the *CDRs,* and the *Federación,* and the Party were paying off. Until the day I heard her screaming in the *patio,* swearing black and blue.

"Who was the son of a bitch who reported me?" she asked out loud, spitting all her anger. Since that day, Elvirita would look at all of us, including me, with mistrust.

"I didn't do it!" I swore, "Why in the hell would I want to report you?"

"If I get my hands on the person who has done it..." Elvirita didn't finish her sentence but she twisted both hands in opposite direction like wringing an invisible neck.

Poor Elvira! She would have to pay the $1000 to *Vivienda* for breaking the law, and the student who was living in her house at the moment, a girl from Panama named Candelaria Martínez, would have to find a legal and much more expensive place to live.

Candelaria Martínez wasn't an ordinary student. She was a historian and a writer who knew exactly how to take advantage of the circumstances that life offered, and how to manipulate fantasy to make it reality and reality to make it fantasy.

"Angelina Martínez and Candelaria Martínez. Um... What a coincidence that the two of us have the same last name!" Candelaria thought determined to use that twist of fate to fight a battle against what she referred to as "The Cuban surrealism."

"I'll be right back!" she announced taking a piece of paper, a pen, and a box full of black and white pictures that Angelina kept in her old *escaparate.*

For several days, Candelaria studied those pictures and made notes with names and last names and dates that went back to the beginning of the 19th century. When Candelaria came out of her confinement, she had created a perfect genealogical tree of the Martínez family from Panama and Cuba.

"Good morning, *Doña*...!

"My name is Adela, Adela Iglesias."

"Good morning, *Doña* Adela. Come in, please!" Candelaria greeted the officer from *Vivienda* who came to Angelina's house to charge the $1000 fine, "My aunt will come in a minute, she went to get the bread at *la bodega*. Can I get you anything? Coffee? Mango juice?"

"A little bit of coffee would be great."

"I am so sorry about all this confusion, *compañera*," Candelaria said trying to be as Cuban as possible, not knowing that Adela would have preferred the title *Doña* rather than *compañera*." It's all my fault! When I arrived, I should have presented my passport to the president of the *CDR* to avoid all this trouble. Whoever denounced my aunt didn't know I'm her niece. I'll go to immigration if it's necessary."

"Can I see your passport?"

"Of course, wait a moment. Look, my aunt is coming. ¡Hola tía! This is the *compañera* who came to talk to us from *Vivienda*. I am so sorry, aunt; I could have avoided all this trouble, but I swear I didn't know that I should have presented my papers to the *CDR*. Please, *compañera*, try these chocolates that I brought my aunt from Panama."

Elvirita was so nervous that she couldn't remember if young Candelaria was her great-grandmother, her sister-in-law, or her fairy godmother, but she managed to reach the hand of the *compañera* saying "These 30 dollars are for you to buy some cream cheese for your children, *compañera*."

Candelaria did the rest of the talking.

"We've asked my aunt one hundred times to come and visit us in Panama, but she loves it here too much, I guess. Now, she says that she is too old to travel, but when she was younger my mother begged her to go and stay with us for a while in Panama City where we live, but she always found an excuse. I came in person to see if I can encourage her to visit us, but she is as stubborn as always."

That was a stupid conversation, anyhow. In Cuba, we all knew that not even invited by the Roman Pope could a person leave the island to freely travel abroad. But Candelaria didn't know and shouldn't haven known that. She took the invented family tree of the Martínez family from Panama and Cuba and pointing to a name she said with a candid and convincing voice:

"When my uncle Marcelo was alive, we thought that he would push her to come visit, but after he died we gave up hope. That's why I am here. If my aunt doesn't visit us, we have to visit her. Sooner or later, all of us will come to Havana to visit her. But I promise that as soon as we arrive, we will present our passport to the president of the *CDR*."

"Well, I'd better go now!" the *compañera* from the Ministry said without even showing the piece of paper with the $1000 fine, "I have other visits to do."

"We apologize for making such a big deal for nothing. I was very ignorant of Cuban law, but I've learned my lesson. It will not happen again, I promise," Candelaria said smiling and shaking hands with the *compañera*. Elvirita said later that she saw how the *compañera* pressed the pocket of her blue uniform to make sure she still had the 30 dollars; her salary of three months!

Since that day, Elvirita and Candelaria became inseparable. Candelaria took her passport to the president of the *CDR* who examined it meticulously, with uneasiness and suspicion, but who didn't have any evidence indicating that the girl was in fact an impostor. Feeling confident about her success with the officer from *Vivienda*, Candelaria even dared to go to Immigration to legalize her status in Cuba as Elvirita's neece.

"Next time, *compañera*" the immigration officer said, "instead of requesting a tourist visa as you have done this time, you must request a family visa so you can stay longer visiting your aunt."

"I'll do that officer. This time I didn't know. I'm very grateful to all of you who have helped me understand how things work here."

When they left the Immigration office, Elvirita noticed that she had pooped her underwear, while Candelaria felt victorious, as she had defeated the Cuban surrealism.

As for me, I had no inheritance from Spain and no possibility to rent a room in my already too crowded apartment, so I kept taking my *meprobamato* to make it easier. But it wasn't easy *caballero*! It wasn't easy! In spite of all the problems and scarcities we had, and in spite of all my worries, fears, and concerns, I felt my body changing and I sensed deeply inside the necessity of a male body close to mine. Day after day I had a burning feeling between my legs, a desire for a man's hand to stroke my breast, and a sadness and a nervousness I couldn't control, not even with the *meprobamato*.

"Is this normal, Caridad?" I asked my family doctor, "I have been separated for a few years now. I am embarrassed about these feelings I have."

"This is totally normal," she said. "You are a woman, and you have to acknowledge that you, and all of us, are sexual beings. You're still young and beautiful. You have to find a boyfriend," she prescribed.

I had the need for intimacy, for words of love, for care, for tenderness, for kisses on my lips, for my skin to be caressed. But I had little respect for men and no time or desire to find a boyfriend. To consol my emptiness, I started rubbing my vulva with a hand. Then with a finger I looked for something I wasn't sure where it was, and the same voice came to my mind every time.

"Do you touch yourself, Rosita?"

"Yes, Father!"

"You shouldn't touch yourself or you will go directly to hell. Where do you touch?"

"I touch my legs and my arms, and my face," I felt ashamed to say that I had also to touch my butt to wipe it off."

"Where else do you touch?"

"Forgive me Father, I touch everywhere."

How in the hell could I survive without touching my body?

The voice of Father Asclepio haunted me and prevented me from finding with my fingers the source of pleasure I had found with Anselmo.

With pleasure or no pleasure, life went on. Before I got entangled in the spider web of the black market, I started sewing school uniforms to all my neighbors. I also did baby sitting, and I managed to open a tiny hairdressing salon for Mima in the living room. But we received just a few *pesos* for all of that because the people we served were as peniless as we were.

I thought about opening a *paladar*, a small restaurant in my living room, that would be more profitable than the hair salon. Maybe, Mima could cook while I served the tables. Mayda could send us *fulas* from *El Norte* to buy the three tables and twelve chairs that the government allowed for *paladares*. But the reality was that in our apartment we couldn't even fit in the furniture for our family. Besides, the toilet hadn't worked since I could remember, and we needed a working toilet to open a *paladar*.

If I couldn't sell inside what Mima cooked, I would sell it outside; I was determined to do whatever it would take to have a more decent living and improve our lives so my children would be happier staying in Cuba.

By that time, Isa had remarried. What a surprise when she told us that she had married *¡un prieto!* Although I have to acknowledge that Leonardo was so charming and clean that he could pass as a white.

My first reaction wasn't good.

"You and your racism!" she yelled furiously at me, "Are you the same person who says the Revolution hasn't taught your children anything? Didn't the Revolution teach you that whites and blacks are all equal?

"Black only for my shoes!" I answered, still yelling.

It was true that *El Comandante* had eliminated the institutional racism from the Island, thinking that we would achieve the category of a raceless society and that racism would be totally eradicated. What a mistake to think in those terms! Blacks would never be like whites! It wasn't only me who thought that way; all of us blacks and whites alike were racists. For me, blacks were rude, always talking loudly and using bad words. Isa had several mulatto friends, but to have a black husband was something else. For a moment, I thought it was a joke, but when she told me they had already married, the only thing I thought was that if Isabel could have *un vientre limpio*,[75] otherwise I would be *peinando trencitas*[76] for the rest of my life. I couldn't imagine myself having a black grandchild. Thank God their son Tonito was born even whiter than Camila.

---

75. To be able to bear a white child despite the black genes of the baby's father.
76. Combing, braiding, and trying to manage the curly hair of a black girl.

Chapter 13
CUBA NoVa

The downfall of Katinka Yushchenko began when the Russian language disappeared from the Cuban educational system. Who wanted to learn Russian in the 90's? Students demanded Italian, Portuguese, French, German, and above all the languages of the enemy, the worst and most dangerous: English.

Katinka, without a job and without communication with her relatives from Ukraine, the once Russian princess, had become a pauper in a foreign country. More than twenty years living in the Island wouldn't make Kati feel totally Cuban, although she couldn't feel totally Russian either. Before she entered a deep state of sadness, Kati rummaged around in her memory trying to uncover her buried native language to sing a lulaby to her newborn grandchild, but she couldn't put two words together in Ukranian. Lost in her own world, feeling unwanted, alien, and isolated, Katinka sat in a rocking chair moving back and forth, swearing in Russian and giving speeches to invisible audiences about the glorious memories of Lenin and Stalin.

It wasn't easy!

Until the day Kati became too ill to stand and even to rock back and ford on her chair.

"It's terminal pancreatitis," the doctor diagnosed and put Kati in the intensive care unit, "It can be a matter of days."

"She isn't going to die," Baltasar assured us after reading the coconuts, "Her grandmother is pulling the cord. You have to do what I say."

"But..." I started arguing.

"A blood relative must cook Kati's grandmother's favorite meal and offer it to her taking it to the cemetery where she is buried."

"But..." I attempted again.

"This must be done before dawn tomorrow. Furthermore, take a raw egg and rub it all over Kati's body saying this prayer," he said giving me a piece of old yellow paper with something written I couldn't understand, "After that, you throw the egg far away in a distant place, as far as you can walk in one day."

It seemed unreasonable, irrational, upsetting, nonsense. But... What if Baltasar was right? I had no choice other than to try to find a blood relative of Kati who would do what I said without asking many questions. It wasn't easy! I convinced Luisito who spoke Russian to call Kati's mom in the Ukraine. Meanwhile I put an egg on my purse and walked to the hospital with my legs shaking and my head spinning. I hesitated at the door, how could I rub an egg over Kati's body if she was in intensive care?

"¡Compañera!" a nurse called me, "Are you coming to see Katinka Yushchenko? Where is the egg? Come on, there is no time!"

Astonished, I handed her the egg.

"Baltasar called me," she said, "It's not the first time," she explained rubbing the egg with energy and concentration over Kati's body saying a prayer without the need of the written one."

"Baltasar thought you would never do it," she confessed.

Two days later Kati was back in her rocking chair. Not only her pancreatitis was gone but also her depression. This time Kati didn't thank Marxism but the African Orishas that saved her life and brought her back to the world of the well and the living. Her price? As the daughter of *Ochún*, Kati had been called to become a *santera*.

While Katinka learned the wonders of her new faith and waited for the rebirth of Russian Communism in the Island, Pipo was dying in *El Norte*. The same morning he died, I looked into the mirror and the person I expected to see wasn't there anymore. For many years I had been moments away from entering the psychiatric hospital of *Mazorra*. Time had passed, first weeks, later months, and then years. I saw sequences of my life passing by as a reflection in the mirror. My life! A little bit more than a list of revolutionary tasks to accomplish! I had a hard time recognizing myself, as my face had no expression.

After that day, a new self-emerged with its own agenda. I regained my own mind, or maybe I created a new one, a combatant mind that wasn't going to fight defending the Revolution anymore. I had my own war to fight, my own battle to win, and I was determined to end up victorious before I died. For the sake of my children and my grandchildren, *¡Venceremos!*

Things that were essential for daily life like vegetable oil, body soap, and laundry detergent among many others were not available through the ration card anymore and were extremely expensive at the *chopin* stores, and with my retirement in Cuban *pesos*, it was impossible to afford any of those products. One pound of powder milk cost $1.00, and my salary when converted into dollars was around $9.00.

It was 1996, Year of the Fall in Combat of Antonio Maceo, and the first thing I had to do was to learn entrepreneurship. In the black market *resolví*[77] some extra flour and coffee, and I started selling cookies at 1 *peso* and the coffee at half of a *peso*. When I was able to get powdered milk in the black market, besides the cookies I made shakes of *fruta bomba* for 2 *pesos*.

Little by little I became more experienced. In the morning I offered all sorts of cookies and shakes, always depending on what I could get in the black market. Many products weren't easy to get because the government had an intense control, especially over

---

77. To manage to do something. In this case, to manage to get extra food.

milk, coffee, and beef. But I developed my strategies to get the best of the best obtainable. I got several providers who were willing to risk their lives to get what the demand wanted.

"Rafael!" María Antonia shouted from outside the coffee factory where her contact was working.

"¡Compañera! Move forward, you can't be here!" the police guarding the place yelled, "Come on move, or I'll arrest you!" he threatened.

"It will be just a moment, *compañero,* I have to say something important to my husband. Rafael! Rafael!"

"I give you three minutes."

When Rafael showed his face out of the window, he made sure the police had directed his attention elsewhere and threw María Antonia a bag full of coffee; a very risky operation that could have cost them both several years in prison.

I learned how to differentiate a good product from a bad one. The black market was not a joke; one could die from adulterated stuff. One time, 14 people died in the province of Matanzas. The news declared that it was an act of sabotage. The archbishop of Havana explained, however, that the man who sold the *frituritas* used sulfuric acid instead of salt because he did not have salt and needed to sell his product.

"Never buy powdered milk that is all white," María Antonia said to me, "Because it has been adulterated with talc or white powder lime. Buy the milk that is yellow, but taste it first. Rub a little bit of the powder with your fingers to see its consistency. Try it and see if it tastes like cream."

Searching the black market took me hours and hours of figuring out how to network. Although when I became more experienced, I didn't have to go to the black market because the black market came to my door.

"*Compañera*, would you like to buy some eggs?" I heard a woman saying behind the door not yet unlocked.

"You must be careful!" I said to the black woman, "A minute ago, I saw a couple of policemen at the corner of the block."

"Oh, yes, I know, I've seen them too. It will take us just a minute."

She was coming from Ramiro's house, who was at the time the delegate of the Communist Party of our block.

"*El compañero* Ramiro told me that you would be interested in buying eggs."

"Yes, sure, come on in. Give me two dozen."

"I am out of here. I am going to pick up my son from the *Círculo*. Today I sold already twenty three dozen eggs. It was a good day."

From that day onward, Doraldina would come to my house every week to sell not only eggs but also whatever she had stolen from the state that day, or whatever she bought from others and was trying to resell. One day I bought from her the whole leg of a pig. Only God knows where she got it. Doraldina also used my house as a rest place after a long working day. We both had coffee together and through her stories of stealing, buying, and selling I became more acquainted with capitalism than I had ever been before. "After all, black people are very resourcefull and smar." I thought.

There was a time when I couldn't find powdered milk anywhere in Havana, not even Doraldina could provide it. Then another strategy came to my mind. I would ask my family doctor for a certificate requesting a special diet for Mima. My wonderful doctor Caridad, not only signed a medical certificate stating that Mima was a diabetic but another one for me saying that I suffered from a stomach ulcer. I took the certificates to the *OFICODA* and we both started receiving powdered milk as a necessary supplement to our diets.

Subsistence became more important than obedience and when people are hungry, there is no law that can't be broken. Most of us in Havana found ways to acquire whatever we needed, even beef, of which even simple possession was extremely penalized. Every other week, a friend of ours who was also a member of the Party provided us with cow meat that he would buy from another member of the Party who in turn had contact with somebody else who... the chain could be endless.

All sectors of our society became, one way or another, involved in the black market. Factories, schools, pharmacies, hospitals, stores, clinics, and offices became involved in the black market. Although the *CDRs*, and the *Federación* still functioned as mechanisms of social control, we all had been trained for years within the system and had learned how to undermine their effectiveness.

Mima and I also kept track of the medicines that were available in the pharmacy. We waited in the morning making a line at the pharmacy, until Adela, the pharmacist, came and told us what was available that day. Whatever was available we took it, then we went to see Caridad again and asked her for the prescription for those medicines. Both Adela and Caridad knew well what Mima and I were doing, but all of us were in the same boat after all. In turn, Caridad would come to my house for coffee almost every day after work, probably the only coffee she had had that day. She also kept vaccines and other stuff in my refrigerator because she didn't have one at the clinic. Adela came to my house every Friday so Mima could fix her nails, and I would sew the uniforms of her children, everything for free. Some people would call all this the black market because we acquired products stolen from the state since everything in Cuba belonged to the government, but for us it wasn't black market but a way to help each other in times of severe necessity.

Almost as scary as the lack of food, was to see how isolated from the rest of the world we were. Cuba was alone, so vulnerable without the Soviets! More than ever before, we had to prepare ourselves, like we did in the 60s, against the most feared enemy of all, the United States. We did many rehearsals to evacuate to the tunnels, organized by areas of Havana; every district had its own tunnel. To protect citizens became one of the main responsibilities of the *CDRs*. In every meeting of the *CDR*, we had to address the issue of civil security. The *CDRs* did a terrific job making sure the civil population would be safe in case of an attack. The president reminded neighbors of the location of the tunnel in case of invasion. The words terrorism and sabotage became common again. We were obsessed with a U.S. attack, not only by air or by boat but we also thought that American agents and spies had infiltrated in our own neighborhoods. I felt the same fear I had felt back in the 60s when Amalita was doing counterrevolution. But this time, my fear was more intense, maybe because I was more conscious about the dangers and also because I had many more responsibilities than I had back then.

The meetings of the *CDR* became a battleground and a source of panic for me and other neighbors.

"*Compañero presidente*," a neighbor would say, "I have to denounce that the garbage containers of the corner of the street are always overloaded with garbage, even right after the *compañeros* of the trash service had cleaned them."

"We are aware of that," the *compañero presidente* answered, "There are undesirable groups of people working in brigades to disturb the population and to destabilize order. They have been hired by the enemy and are in charge of bringing garbage so we develop vectors of diseases in our neighborhood. Rats, and cockroaches will do the rest. The *Poder Popular* is doing its best to protect us all, and so far everything is under control."

Another neighbor would complain about the *buzos,* men, women, elderly, disturb people, youth who looked for food inside the garbage containers; they literally dived in the trash searching for edible stuff.

"These people are not what they seem," the president informed, "They are not poor people. They are secret agents sent by the CIA and paid by the Americans to deceive us all that there is hunger among the Cuban people. *Buzos* also work in brigades to keep the streets dirty and to create potential vectors for disease."

"With your permission, *compañero presidente,* this isn't true!" a neighbor dared to say, "These are just excuses to avoid the real problem. Nobody wants to admit that we live in underdevelopment and that there is poverty and hunger, and that there are people in Havana who need to find their food in garbage containers because there is no food anywhere."

"Yes!" shouted another neighbor, "It's easier to blame the United States than to confront our own mistakes."

I was astonished to hear such accusations in public. I started sweating in fright.

"The United States wants to terrify the Island, this is nothing new and we all know it!" another yelled defending the president's position.

"You can't tell me that the people who pee and shit inside my building are sent by the United States because I don't buy it."

"You better do, *compañera!*" the president insisted trying to control himself, "I have proof of that. Men who urinate and defecate in the hallway of apartment buildings have been sent by the United States to cause odor and dirtiness. Furthermore, I can also tell you that the death of two trees across the street has been caused by a virus sent by the Cuban-Americans of Miami."

My fear was not just the United States or the Cuban-Americans. I had fear of everything: of seeing my children and grandchildren starving and dying, of witnessing that my relatives or friends would take a raft and leave the Island, of losing my mind. I had the fear of being haunted by fear.

In 1996 Mayda came back to Havana again. Bad times to return to the Motherland.

"This city looks like Beirut," she said on her way home along Rancho Boyeros, "Havana reminds me of a television program I saw years ago showing the destruction of the city after the war in Lebanon."

It was true. Havana was falling apart, but the deterioration had been so slow and steady that those of us who lived in the city couldn't even see it; we couldn's see the debris, the garbage, and the dirtiness anymore; we had gotten used to living in misery and destruction.

The most impressing feeling for Mayda was to see homeless people living in the debris, with no water or electricity.

"Most are *marginales*," I was prompted to say before she could draw any conclusions, "Black people with many children who have choosen to live that way. The Revolution provides shelters for them, you know, but they refuse."

"So much coercion, suffering, and endurance on the part of Cubans, for God's sake," she whispered.

Maydita again became the savior of my family. No more need of the black market while she was in Havana. She filled with groceries our ancestral friend Willy that had been working since the 50's. God bless that refrigerator. Mayda also brought school supplies for Camila and disposable diapers for newborn Tonito.

"¡Caballero!" Mayda exclaimed, after seeing that Isabel reused over and over again the disposable diapers, "You people are the masters of recycling. In the United States, we have so much to learn from you."

Isa had made a little incision on every diaper, and when it was soaked she would take the inside wet material out, wash the outside part and replace the inside again with a clean and thick layer of cotton she bought at the pharmacy for Cubans. One package of twenty-seven diapers could last six or seven months. Isa even washed the soiled diapers that weren't too messy.

As it happened the first time, Mayda's visit wasn't easy. It took a lot out of me to take her charity. Besides, we had our differences, who wouldn't after almost 30 years of forced forgetfulness? Again, we both needed to ease our resentments and guilt, sometimes her money helped and sometimes it made it worse. I loved Maydita to death but I had many mixed feelings not only about taking her *fulas* but also about the way neighbors and family received her. Was I jealous? It seemed to me that everybody, including the state, welcomed her and treated her better than they treated me after having devoted my entire life to fight for the Revolution defending its ideals all the days and nights of forty long years. It was devastating to realize that I was unwanted in my own country while my sister had become a goddess worshiped by the same Revolution she had betrayed.

"Let's take a trip and visit our relatives in Pinar del Río and Matazas," Mayda suggested one day, "I'll rent a car."

"¡Chévere!" we said all excited. In my ignorance, I tought that Isa and I would go to the *Habana Libre* hotel to rent the car because Mayda didn't know how things worked in Havana anymore; and so we did. There we went Isa and I with Mayda's *fulas* in our pockets, feeling important and rich. I had never been inside a hotel for foreigners because Cubans were not allowed to enter those kinds of hotels. We had our own ones where the toilets never flushed and water never came out of the faucets. We had never been allowed to speak with foreigners either. The only foreigners we knew were the ones who had arrived from the allied socialist countries and from Africa; there were Palestinians as well.

I felt nervous and anxious as we approached the *Habana Libre*. The guards at the door had been well trained to kick out Cubans who were close to the hotel. What about if they did that to us? What an embarrassment!

The guard didn't stop us. In the lobby I was paralyzed. I couldn't believe all that luxury in a hotel, so clean and shiny.

"Good morning *compañera*," I said at the counter of the car rental, "We want to rent a small car."

"I need to see the passport of the *señora*" referring to Isa.

"Her what?"

"I need to see her passport!" she explained impatiently and almost shouting.

"We have our Cuban IDs! Would you like to see them?"

"Ah, so both of you are Cubaaan!" she said with disgust. "I am sorry *compañera*. We can only rent cars to foreigners and neither of you is a foreigner."

Then Isa talked, "Look lady, I have my own passport because I went to Europe, but I don't have it with me because I never thought I would need a passport in my own country."

"You don't get it *compañera,* do you? I don't want to see your Cuban passport. I need a foreign passport. What part you don't understand?"

"But, we have American dollars. I don't understand. If we have the money, why can't we rent a car?"

"There is nothing I can do for you, *compañera*. Cubans can't rent cars."

"This system is finishing us all!" Isa shouted almost crying in the street.

We went back home without the car. Hours later, we returned to the hotel with Mayda. She showed her American passport and we got the car!! I was so sorry for Isa, I was so sorry for myself. I felt the humiliation way beyond my physical body, I felt my soul shattered. My sister Mayda, the deserter, the garbage, the gusana, had become the privileged person in Cuba again, this time because she had acquired the nationality of the enemy. It didn't make sense to me. Mayda was treated like a queen wherever she went while the rest of us were nothing more than her shadow. That hurt me deeply and destroyed my hope that all our sacrifices and struggles would help us achieve a more prosperous life. My sister could get a taxi but I couldn't go in the same taxi with her. My sister could enter a restaurant but I couldn't eat with her at her table, I couldn't even get inside the same restaurant. The glory had been reserved for those who were once considered enemies of the state. The misery was meant for us authentic revolutionaries.

When Mayda left, I decided to make a living of my own and never depend on my sister's charity. I needed dollars! Selling cookies and coffee and fixing nails wasn't enough. Camila's fifteenth birthday party would come in less than two years and I needed to find a way to earn dollars and save money for that.

It wasn't easy. Jobs that paid in dollars were scarce and Cubans fought for them tooth and nails. There was a kind a mafia around the hotels and restaurants for foreigners. A position for a cleaning lady at the hotel *Habana Libre* cost $1,000. That is, a person would have to save that kind of money to have access to a cleaning position there. How could I get $1000 just to apply for a cleaning job?

I heard a rumor that some foreigners, mostly from Spain, had bought houses in Havana, illegally of course, and were in need of domestic service. If I wanted dollars, I knew I couldn't work in the house of a Cuban who would pay in pesos.

Everybody had an opinion about my decision to work as a domestic.

"All these years of revolutionary life to end servitude and now you want to be a maid? You're not in your right mind, Rosi." Mima reprimanded me.

"What a contradiction and irony!" Isa said.

"You see, the Revolution has been good for nothing. Forty stupid years of suffering for what?" Pedrito insisted.

Until the day somebody told me about a wealthy Spaniard who urgently needed a maid. I went to see him.

Señor Sergio had a big house in Kholy, one of the wealthiest neighborhoods of Havana. As I would find out later, he bought the house at a very low price and registered it under the name of his Cuban butler with the hope that after the Revolution he could change the name and become the sole owner of the house.

At his house, *señor* Sergio hosted many important parties and dinners, especially for foreign businessmen and for Cuban government officials. Ministers and even Raúl[78] had been guests of *señor* Sergio. In the house, there was a butler, a driver, a gardener, and three maids, one of whom had become ill and needed to be replaced as soon as possible because some important members of the Party and people from Spain were about to pay a visit.

The day I had my interview, *señor* Sergio seemed somewhat nervous. He was tall, handsome, had graying hair, beard and mustache, along with the prominent belly of those who are well fed. He said he was from an island in Spain. Needless to say, I was also shaking of nervousness.

"From *Isla Galicia*?" Another maid asked him.

"No, no, from Mayorca," he said.

What a shame! Forty years of a good educational system and Cubans still didn't know any geography at all.

"In the old times, I would have required you to wear a uniform," *señor* Sergio said to me, "Now it's different. I feel uneasy to ask my maids to wear a uniform living in a communist country, but cloth etiquette is very important in this house, and even more for you because you will need to serve the table to high dignitaries. My driver, butler, and gardener also wear uniforms. If you work for me, will you be willing to wear a European style black and white maid uniform?"

"How much would you pay? Do you pay in *pesos* or in dollars?"

---

78. Referring to Raúl Castro.

"I pay in dollars. My maids get $100 a month."

One hundred dollars! I couldn't believe what I just heard. I would be earning three times the salary of a good surgeon in Cuba and almost four times what Anselmo got for his job at the hospital.

"For 100 dollars, I would wear a uniform and whatever else you want me to wear." I answered still amazed at the salary of a maid in communist Cuba, "You've got your maid, *señor*."

Chapter 14

WHEN GOD CAME INTO HAVANA

"Rosi, Rosi, Rosi!" my neighbor Elvira called hysterically, "I had a phone call for you from Cienfuegos saying that Anselmo is very ill."

Anselmo wasn't ill, he was dead. He had suffered a heart attack while he was in bed with a nineteen-year-old *mulata*. It seems that Anselmo took advantage of the proliferation of *jineteras* and *pingueros* in Havana during the *Período Especial* and instead of sleeping with nurses and secretaries as he had done before, he went around El Vedado to select a girl for a night or a weekend. I was surprised, though, since prostitutes targeted foreigners instead of nationals.

"God have mercy on this poor sinner!" Mima prayed for him.

"Poor girl!" Isa said with a mixture of sadness and disgust, "A teenager with a dirty old guy. This is what necessity brings."

"How can you call her poor girl?" I said angrily, "These girls aren't poor. They are selfish and shameless, with no scruples to get what they want. The government provides for them but they want fancy stuff. They would sleep with their own fathers to drink a Coca-Cola or to buy a bottle of European perfume."

Pedrito and Boris respected their father and mourned his death until the day we put Anselmo in the ground at the Colón cemetery, there they met face-to face a fifteen-year-old girl and a six-year-old boy from different mothers who apparently shared the same father with my children.

On January 21 1998, Year of the Fortieth Anniversary of the Decisive Battles of the Liberation War, a few months after Anselmo was buried, John Paul II kissed the land of Cuba and the whole fuss around the Pope's visit helped my children to forget the pain and humiliation of their father's life and death.

I took Mima and Camila to the street to welcome the Pope. The three of us waved Cuban flags, and Camila wore a blue T-shirt and a hat with the image of the Pope.

The expectation before the Pope's arrival was unbelievable. Many Cubans even thought that the Holy Father would end the *Período Especial*, solve all our economic problems, and change the system for good.

Pedrito believed people had absurd expectations, "Not even God can solve what the devil has created in the Island," he said.

"The Pope will probably say things Cubans want to hear," said Isa, "We all need somebody with his authority to tell us that we have to trust, to have hope in the future, and to help each other; things like that."

"If the Pope doesn't bring rice and black beans to the people, they will soon forget that John Paul was ever here," Boris said.

Katinka was the only one among us who had a strong negative opinion about the Pope's visit. She saw the event as an insult, believing that he would sweep away the last vestiges of Communism on the Island.

Some people had no opinion and just made jokes about the visit.

"Do you know why John Paul II is coming to Cuba"?

"To bring hope in the future, I guess."

"Nope! He is coming to see three things he has never seen before: first, to see a camel in the Tropics, second to see how a country lives out of miracle, and finally to meet the devil on Earth."

I couldn't help but to be excited. I cleaned the dust from Mima's old shrine and made offerings to San Lázaro and *la Caridad del Cobre*. Mima was more alert than ever, the Pope's visit meant for her that God had finally chosen the people of Cuba. She found her rosary and took it with her everywhere, even when she went to the bodega and the agro.

The Pope said a mass at the *Plaza de la Revolución*. At one side of the square, the gigantic face of *Ché* on the front of the Ministry of Interior, at another side of the square, attached at the wall of the National Library, an enormous image of the Sacred Heart. Huge banners everywhere greeted Karol Wojtyla: "Welcome John Paul II, messenger of Truth and Hope."

There we went to the square, to the *Plaza de la Revolución*. In thirty years I hadn't felt so alive, so happy, and so enthusiastic, like I felt during the first months of the Revolution. The Pope criticized neoliberalism, the system that according to *El Comandante* made the rich richer and the poor poorer. He condemned the government of *El Norte* and its absurd embargo against our Island. He exalted the figure of our legendary *Che* Guevara. But he also asked for the fulfillment of human rights in Cuba and strongly condemned Marxism, and proposed a Christian revolution instead of an atheist one. After Communion, Fidel shook hands with priests and nuns while millions of us watched and held our breaths in expectation. We shook hands with each other in collective hysteria. All Cubans united again by the desire to live a better life, a decent life, a freer life. Although <u>Granma</u> said that 250,000 or 300,000 Cubans were at the Mass, I could swear there were several millions.

We were again in the streets expressing our hopes and dreams. Daily frustrations would turn into fulfillment and scarcity would eventually turn into prosperity. The levels of energy and hope were incredible. The Pope's visit could only be compared with the first arrival of the *barbudos* to Havana. In both occasions, we Cubans thought that the world was turning around us and that the future of Cuba would drastically change.

With Fidel, Mima had thought that a messenger of God had come to the Island. With the Pope, she believed that God himself had finally decided to have mercy on us. There was a difference between the two moments, though. With Fidel, the collective euphoria was exaggerated and there was no space for uncertainty. With the Pope's visit, there was also a lot of skepticism and disbelief. Maybe after all those years, people had learned that there was a difference between what it appears to be and what it really is.

On January 26, the Pope left the Island leaving behind optimism and hope for many and doubt and mistrust for some. The Pope's words were interpreted according to the needs and expectations of each group and each individual. For Kati, the essential part of Karol Wojtyla's visit was that he denounced neoliberalism and the U.S. embargo against Cuba. For Boris and Pedrito, John Paul II came to Cuba to claim more freedom and human rights. Mima understood that the Pope's strongest point was against atheism. Isabel's desire to travel around the world made her believe that the most important part of the visit was when the Pope asked "That Cuba opens to the world and that the world opens to Cuba." In any case, we all clearly needed faith to face the crisis and overcome the many difficulties we had.

After the Pope's visit, more Cubans than ever before turned to religion instead of to politics or ideology. It seemed as if our *Fidelismo* had pragmatically incorporated Christianity. Mima would continue to take her rosary everywhere, and I started attending Sunday Mass. Meanwhile, *El Comandante* had also channeled the increasingly restlessness of Cuban youth towards the figure of *Ché* Guevara as a reinforcement for their revolutionary ideology. In fact, in the summer of 1998, the Pope and *Ché* were the two most popular figures among Camila's group of friends.

"Fidel is using *Ché* and Camilo to control the young," Pedrito said.

"Maybe Camila's generation is the only one that can change the path of history again, the one that can revolutionize this Revolution," Isabelita commented.

Besides renewed hope and enthusiasm, Karol Wojtyla brought more willingness to openly talk about themes that had been hidden for decades. The Pope, however, as Boris had predicted, did not bring rice and black beans to the Cuban population, neither did he bring substantial changes for Cuban society. One big change was that after the Pope left the Island, Fidel liberated 299 political prisoners as John Paul II had requested, and another 224 for humanitarian reasons. Another change was that Christmas Day was declared a national holiday again. However, daily life for Cubans continued to be as it was before the Pope's visit. Some remained loyal to the Revolution, and some kept building rafts to abandon the land that had given them everything and beyond.

People kept dying at sea almost every day. The lucky ones managed to reach the coast of the United States, or were sent to Guantánamo Bay and waited in a legal limbo for months or even years. None of them, however, deserved a space in the news: deserters, hypocrites, selfish people always thinking about their own well being. Until one day of November 1999, Year of the Fortieth Anniversary of the Triumph of the Revolution, that a little boy from Cárdenas named Elián González cheated Fortune and was found floating on an inner tube off the Florida coast after the small aluminum boat sank killing his mother and 10 more people. Three, including Elián, survived, but only the five-year old Elián would make big news creating an international storm and chaos on the Island.

"Elián González has been rescued by American fishermen and is now safely living with his great-uncle in Miami's Little Havana district. He will be better off in the United States, as his mother had dreamed, than in Cuba," *Radio Martí* stated.

"The mother of Elián, Elizabeth Brotons, kidnapped the child against the will of Elián's father and was taken illegally from

Cuba," said our national TV, "He must be returned to his homeland immediately. This is another American attempt to destroy the dignity of our people."

"Elián González made it to the United States thanks to his mother who sacrificed her life for the sake of her son. The child deserves to live in freedom, far away from the longest and most cruel communist dictatorship in the history of humankind." *Radio Martí* again.

"Elián is the son of all Cubans and must be returned to us, to the land of freedom, the land that fought for the equality of all humans, the land of justice for all, his homeland," again the national news.

"The United States are protecting the rights of the child," *Radio Martí*.

"The United States are violating the most fundamental human right of Elián González," national news.

"Juan Miguel González, Elián's father, is being manipulated by Castro's regime with the same old and dirty techniques that have been used for decades to coerce people's free will."

"Elián's father, Juan Miguel González, declared that the extremist mafia of Miami attempted to bribe him with two million dollars if he agrees to go to Miami and seek asylum in the United States."

"A video has been released in which Elián tells Juan Miguel that he wants to stay in the United States."

"In that video, Elián has been coached, as a male voice can be heard off-camera directing the boy."

"Attorney General Janet Reno has ordered the return of Elián to his father but the Miami relatives have defied the order. Negotiations will continue."

"There is no negotiation. The anti-Cuban mafia of Florida must return Elián to Cuba. Our values and principles are not negotiable."

"For several days, Elián's house in Miami has been surrounded by protesters as well as police. The relatives insist that Elián will not be returned to Cuba. Exile groups discuss plans to form a human chain around the house to prevent federal agents from repatriating him. Some drivers had even begun to block roads by slowly circling the house."

"This is the best example of American absurdity and of the weakness of the Clinton administration that doesn't know how to stop the Miami's extremist right wing."

The dispute over Elián sparked mass demonstrations all over the Island. Combatant open tribunes, heated debates, patriotic round tables, large demonstrations of students, and popular rallies became a daily routine. *El Comandante* led one of the largest mass campaigns in our history, *la Marcha del Pueblo Combatiente*.[79]

"Return Elián to his homeland!" people screamed on the streets.

"Elián, Cuba is reclaiming you!"

"Eleven million Cubans are waiting for you!"

"You will come back to your school, Elián!"

"Freedom for Elián!"

"Is this the same *Comandante* who didn't give a dam for the twelve children who died when the tugboat *13 de Marzo* sank?" Boris said angrily.

"The mother of Elián wanted the best for her son," said Pedrito, "I would have done the same."

"If Elián returns, he will have a much better life here in Cuba than the rest of us. *El Comandante* will provide." Isa said.

---

79. The rally of the combattant country.

"But Eliancito's father has requested his repatriation," Mima said defending the *Patria o Muerte, Venceremos.*

"His father is a coward!" Isa jumped up, "He is saying what the government wants him to say. He's being manipulated, he has no free will."

Finally, one day in April, Elián's father flew to the US with his new wife and baby son, to take Elián back home. Fidel bid farewell to him at the airport in Havana. It would take two more months for Eliancito to be reunited with his father, when American authorities took Elián by force from his Miami relatives.

"Assassins!" yelled some protesters in Miami climbing over the barricades in an attempt to stop the agents, burning garbage containers, tires, and trees. Crowds jammed a more than 10-block area. Police in riot gear were deployed and tear gas was used. Many businesses closed, as their owners and managers participated in a short boycott to support Elián's stay in the United States.

The 28th of June of 2000, Year of the Fortieth Anniversary of the Homeland or Death decision and a few months before Camila turned fifteen, Elián returned to Cuba. Large masses of people waited for him at the airport, on the streets, everywhere.

"Elián! Elián! Elián! Elián! Elián! Elián! Elián!" people shouted in victorious frenzy.

Nothing much changed in our lives with the return of Elián González. Anselmo was gone, my children kept complaining about the situation in Cuba, and I kept working as a maid for *señor* Sergio, dressed in a black and white European uniform.

In a year and a half, I managed to save $1000 for Camila's fifteenth birthday party, the same amount Anselmo and I had flushed down the toilet years ago. Anselmo didn't make that kind of money in all his years of working as a medical doctor. Camila deserved a big fifteen birthday party. She had become a beautiful and happy young lady, a good student attending the best boarding high school in Havana, *la Lenin*[80]. She came home every two weekends, and I visited her at *la beca* the weekends she did not come home. That girl was all my life and I felt closer to her than to any of my children. Camila was the perfect product of our society, the result of forty years of communism in the Island. On the one hand, she wanted to become a doctor, like her grandfather, but she also wanted to learn English and live with her aunt Mayda in El Norte. On the other hand, she wanted to be like *Ché* but would like to have money and a big and beautiful house in Miramar. Camila wanted to get married and have children, but also a maid or two. Her maids, however, would be well paid and treated as a part of the family, *compañeras* who, according to her, would feel fulfilled doing the chores and taking care of the kids.

Camila wanted to be rich. She didn't want to dress as everybody else, or behave as everybody else; she wanted to be different, she wanted to be herself. That attitude, however, wasn't unique to Camila but to a whole generation that wanted to rebel against everything known. It happened at *la Lenin* as well. where all children had to wear uniform, boys and girls, with the idea of keeping it simple and equal. The only thing kids could wear differently was the shoes, but even that little freedom became a source of conflict when some kids whose parents had more access to dollars than others started wearing Adidas and Nike while other kids wore very old and bad quality shoes. Since not all teenagers had access to U.S. dollars, the ones who did used it as a means to assert power and status. They found in the American and Western European goods a way of showing off.

At first, I saw that attitude as a lack of respect, but Isabel said it was a natural way to evolve and go forward.

"Consumerism means progress for the youth, Marxism means backwardness, and communism is too fossilized. The youth are

---

80. *La Lenin* refers to one of the most prestigious high schools in Havana. It was named after Vladimir Illich Lenin. Studying at *la Lenin* was a symbol of prestige and sophistication.

now looking for symbolic power," Isa said using all her psychological knowledge, "Ideology is not a form of power for them anymore, and having a degree and a career doesn't translate into prestige as it did before. What is the point of saving money for a teenager if there is nothing they can invest in? They can't buy a motorcycle or even a bike, and since there is no private property they can't think about buying a house in the future. Buying clothes and whatever is available has become synonymous with economic well being and that's why they desire American and European brands."

"This is not unique to my generation," Camila complained, "I bet that of all you were the same way but you don't remember. The difference is that before the things that you desired came from the socialist countries instead of from the United States or Western Europe."

It was true. Isa and her friends would have died for fancy clothes such as new *pitusas* or panties. When Isa was in first year of college she became a very good friend with the daughter of the Cuban ambassador in Czechoslovakia. That girl invited her to many parties at her house and to the house of other diplomats, and she also brought her many presents from her trips to the Communist bloc. One day, her friend brought her a beautiful *pitusa* and some really modern blouses. Isa wore those clothes every day until they became like rags.

"Now, for me and my friends, there aren't more socialist countries, no more friends in socialism because there is no socialism," Camila said defending herself and her generation. "Whenever you two receive dollars from *Estados Unidos*, the first thing you do is go to the *chopin* and buy groceries. But, we aren't so concerned with food. If I had *fulas*, I would love something by Calvin Klein, Nike, Adidas, Gucci and things like that."

Camila was right. Her mother and I bought groceries first. If we could save something, we left it for emergencies, like going to the pharmacy for foreigners because when we needed medication that wasn't available in our pharmacies, we asked a foreigner to buy the medicine for us in *divisas*.

To celebrate Camila's fifteenth birthday, we rented an old and beautiful house in Guanabacoa, one humid day of December. The big *patio* of the house was full of people and many more kept coming. At 8:00 pm there were probably around 200 guests. Camila was there like a royal figure in her fabulous rented light blue dress; her pictures already had been taken in a room of the same house. There was live music in the *patio*, beverages, and food. Everything seemed so luxurious that for a moment I forgot we were still living in the middle of the *Período Especial* until I saw people devouring their food that was served in a small cardboard boxes: pastries, fried dough, and a piece of cake.

Without anything else to eat, people drank punch, rum with coke, and a green liquor that Pedrito had prepared with extract of mint he took from the laboratory he worked. Two hours later the dance started in the ballroom, a big and beautiful salon. Most of the music came from a boom-box, but there was live music as well. Isa couldn't help crying when she heard "Imagine there's no heaven. It's easy if you try. Imagine all the people…"

Just a week before Camila's party, on December 8th *El Comandante* himself went to greet an almost human statue of John Lennon made in bronze that rested on an iron bench at a park in El Vedado with the name of the singer. Decades before it would have been a heresy to say out loud the name of the ex-Beatles. From that moment on he would join the list of national heroes; Camila and her friends would often wear t-shirts of John Lennon and *Ché* Guevara together. Lennon would never be alone in Havana. He would even have four guardians who took turns day and night to preserve the glasses that the sculptor had screwed to the bronze and that had been stolen several times. The guardians decided to take the glasses off and put them back on when a tourist approached or when somebody wanted to take a picture sitting on the bench by the side of the new hero of Cuba.

"You may say I'm a dreamer but I'm not the only one," a plaque close to Lenon said written in his own caligraphy.

Being an island contributed to our isolation, but I understood right there that no country can close its doors to the world for fear of being contaminated.

"Yesterday, all my troubles seemed so far away. Now it looks as though they're here to stay. Oh I believe in yesterday" came out from the boom-box.

And later, "Let it be, let it be, let it be, let it be. There will be an answer, let it be."

Camila danced first with Pedrito and later with Boris. The party lasted until 3:00 in the morning.

"This has been the most beautiful day of my life," Camila said to me, "I really felt like the whole world danced around me. I felt important, I felt very special. I enjoyed every part of it."

In the pictures, Camila posed with different costumes and in different scenarios. In several pictures she was in the *patio* of the house, sitting close to a fountain and wearing a dark blue dress from the XIX century. In other pictures, she was in a room with some furniture resembling an old fashioned bar wearing a cabaret dancer costume. In some other pictures she was in the same room, wearing a bikini, and with decorations on the wall of a Varadero beach with palm trees. She had other pictures taken in the same room with her coming out from a real bathtub with a towel around her body and another towel covering her long black hair like a turban. All her poses were very sensual, very enticing, and very glamorous.

Next day, we all would have to go through the same struggles as the day before, but for one day we forgot all our miseries; buses that never came, water that didn't run, and food that was never enough to fill us up. We all enjoyed, sang, danced, screamed, got drunk, and felt happy without mentioning either *Revolución* or *Período Especial*.

EPILOGUE

Soon it will be September, the fourth anniversary of Rosa's stroke.

Everything is new and exciting for Camila. She is going to need a few months to adjust, though. She still takes a piece of toilet paper in her pocket wherever she goes, "one never knows" she excuses herself. And the other day she left a librarian at the University of Chicago in state of shock.

"Excuse me, can you tell me where can I find a typewriter?"

"A typewriter?" the librarian asked in disbelief.

"Yes, I need a typewriter."

The librarian disappeared for quite a long time. She came back with an odd expression and a key.

"Go to the second floor, take a right and then a left. The first little room you find has a typewriter. Return the key when you're done, please."

"This university only has one typewriter?" Camila wondered.

"Maybe she needs to write a paper about the mechanism of a typewriter for an archaeology class," the librarian must have thought. Just the following day, Camila discovered a Computer Lab at the University of Chicago; no need for the typewriter, she guessed.

I still don't understand why Camila leaves the faucet open when she is doing the dishes, even when she stops washing to talk for several minutes. To me it appears to be hours seeing the water run, run, and run while she talks on unconcerned about the precious fluid. Or, why she leaves all the lights on when she doesn't need them? It's hard to believe that her mother and grandmother felt sick about not having running water at home and about the blackouts that swept Havana, but Camila seems so indifferent about wasting these costly and valuable items. I have to be patient with her. She was even surprised to find out that I have to pay the water I consume in my house! "Doesn't the government pay for this?" she asked.

Another day she abandoned a city bus when she felt a flat tire.

"*Se jodió la guagua!*"[81] she thought, left and walked three miles home. Two days later, at the first "flat tire" she decided to stay on the bus; a minute later, a lady in a wheelchair came on board and the bus went back up and kept running as before.

"I'm finishing writing your grandmother's story," I tell Camila at dinner.

"My grandmother's story? Why?"

Rosa never thought about why was she telling me her story, she just did. At Sergio's house there was little to do when he wasn't home. During many months of the year, Sergio had several maids working in the house for his permanent guests. It was somewhat natural for the maids to tell and for guests to listen while sitting on the porch waiting for the afternoon heat to pass.

"Cubans don't talk to other Cubans anymore about these things; what would be the point?" Rosa used to say.

When I traveled and left the Island for a while, your grandma Rosa nervously waited for my return.

"I couldn't wait for you to come back. I need to release everything I have inside," she used to say.

"Who would be interested in my grandma's story?"

"You don't think that her story can be published?"

"No way! That would only happen with stories of the big heroines of that time, like Haydée Santamaría, Celia Sánchez, or Tania *la Guerrillera*, or even Vilma Espín, but not with my

---

81. "The bus just got fucked up!"

grandma's. She didn't have an extraordinary life or anything like that. *Abuela* Rosa had a very ordinary life, a life like many others. Who would want to read about the boring life of an ordinary Cuban woman living all her life during the boring Cuban Revolution?"

GLOSSARY

A

Abuela: Grandmother.

Acto de repudio: Act of Repudiation. See Note 17.

Agro: Farmers market.

Agua con azúcar: Sugared water.

Ajustadores: Bra.

Apagón: Electric blackout.

Arrimá: A woman who lives with her partner without being married. The word is a reduction of arrimada, which means to move closer to.

Asamblea de Rendición de Cuentas: Literally meaning Rendering of Accounts Assembly. It refers to electoral districts meetings of neighborhood residents and the regional delegate of the "National Assembly of People's Power" (the legislative parliament of Cuba). In these meetings the representative recounts and explains the decisions taken by the National Assembly of the People's Power, and citizens report problems or ideological deviations in the neighborhood.

Ave, Fidel, Cubans morituri te salutant: Hail, Fidel, Cubans who are about to die salute you. Variant wording of the well-known Latin phrase "*Ave, Caesar, morituri te salutant*" ("Hail, Caesar, those who are about to die salute you").

B

Babalao: Title for the priests of Ifá, a divination system in the Yoruba religion. The *babalao* or *babalawo* ("Father Who Knows the Secrets") is the supreme priest in the syncretic religion known as *Santería* or *Regla de Ocha*. (For *Santería* see Note 16).

Balsa: Raft.

Balsero: Rafter, derived from the word *balsa* (raft).

Barbacoa: Literally meaning grill or barbecue, refers to the platforms built in the high vertical spaces of the houses in Cuba, subdividing and rearranging indoor spaces in order to provide housing for a large number of the Cuban population, as the housing shortage became more acute.

Banco Nacional de Cuba: Cuba National Bank.

Barbudos (los barbudos): Bearded men. Rebel forces of the Cuban Revolution.

Beca (la beca): Boarding School.

Bemba: Thick lips.

Bisabuela: Great-grandmother.

Bisté: Beef steak.

Bloqueo: Embargo.

Blúmer: Cuban word for panties.

Bocadito de frazada: Rag sandwich.

Bodega: Grocery store.

Bodeguero: Sales person at the *bodega* (grocery store).

Bohemia: Popular Cuban magazine published since 1908.

Bola (la bola): Rumor.

Brigadas de Acción Rápida: Rapid Action Brigades, also known as Rapid Response Brigades.

Brigadista: A member of the "literacy brigades" formed in 1961 during the Cuban Literacy Campaign. The word also refers to the members of revolutionary brigades who have the role of civil guards.

Buzos: Literally meaning "scuba divers". In Cuba, the term refers to people who looked or "dived" for food in dumpsters.

C

¡Caballero!: Oh, man!

Calle 23: 23rd Street, also known as *La Rampa*, is the main street of *El Vedado* neighborhood, the downtown of Havana.

CAME: Acronym for *Consejo de Ayuda Mutua Económica*, Council for Mutual Economic Assistance (CMEA or COMECON).

Camello: Trailer buses named camels for their "humps". They circulated in Havana carrying over two hundred passengers during the economic 1990s economic crisis in Cuba.

Campo socialista: Socialist Block.

Carajo: Damn, fuck.

Caridad del Cobre: Virgen of Charity of Copper, Cuba's patroness.

CDR: Acronym for *Comité de Defensa de la Revolución*, Committee for the Defense of the Revolution.

Cederista: A member of the *CDR* or *Comité de Defensa de la Revolución*, Committee for the Defense of the Revolution.

Central: Sugar cane factory.

Círculo infantil (círculo): Day care center.

Cisterna: Water tank.

Ciudad Libertad: Liberty City is a large educational complex in Western Havana. Before 1959 it was known as Columbia, the former headquarters of Fulgencio Batista regime's armed forces.

Cocido madrileño: Spanish stew (from Madrid).

Columbina: Convertible bed for one person.

Comandante (El Comandante, Mi comandante): Commander (The Commander, My Commander), referring to Fidel Castro.

Comité Central: Central Committee of the Communist Party.

Compañero: Comrade.

Comuñangas: Pejorative way to refer to communists.

Condiloma: Condyloma (infection of the genitals).

Conga: Cuban music and dance style, very popular during the carnival season.

Congrí: Typical Cuban dish of rice cooked with black beans.

Contingentes obreros: Construction work contingents.

Contingente Blas Roca: *Blas Roca* Construction Work Contingent. It was created by Fidel Castro as the country's very first work contingent. Named after Blas Roca Calderío (one of the leaders of the Communist Party, and theoreticians of the Cuban Revolution), it is the most famous, distinguished and closest to the president.

Coño: Damn, fuck.

Culero: Cloth diaper.

Chavitos: Slang word for convertible Cuban pesos.

Chévere: Great.

Chico, chica: Girl, boy.

Chopin, Chopi: Stores and shopping centers run by the government. The word comes from the English "shopping".

D

Delegado: Delegate.

Descara'o: Shameless, insolent. The word is a reduction from *descarado*.

Diplo-tienda (diplo): Shopping center for diplomats and foreigners in Cuba.

Divisa: Foreing currency.

Dominicas (las Dominicas): Dominican nuns.

Don: Mr.

Doña: Mrs.

E

El Corte Inglés: The most famous department store chain in Spain, and the biggest store group in Europe. Literally meaning "The English Cut".

El Norte: The North, referring to the United States.

Escaparate: Wardrobe.

Escoria: Scum.

Estados Unidos: United States.

F

Faja: Female underwear.

FAR: Acronym for *Fuerzas Armadas Revolucionarias*, Revolutionary Armed Forces.

Federación: Short for *Federación de Mujeres Cubanas*, Federation of Cuban Women, also referred as *FMC* according to its initials in Spanish.

Federada: A member of the Federation of Cuban Women.

Fidelismo: Left-wing ideology created by Fidel Castro.

Fondillúa: Big-butted woman. The word derives from *fondillo* (butt).

Fósforo vivo: Literally meaning "Living match". It refers to gelatin capsules filled with sulfuric acid, used by the opposition to start fires in public places, destabilizing Fidel Castro's government.

Frente ideológico: Ideological Front

Frente de Recuperación de Valores del Estado: Campaign for the Recovery of State Revenue.

Frigidaire: Refrigerator, taken from the US brand "Frigidaire".

Frituritas: Fried dough.

Frutabomba: Papaya.

Fulas: Slang word for American dollars.

Fusil: Rifle.

G

Gallego: Literally meaning Galician. It is used in Cuba to refer to Spanish people.

Gazpacho andaluz: Cold soup from Andalusia. Gazpacho.

Granma (yacht): The name of the yacht used by Fidel Castro, Ernesto *Che* Guevara and other revolutionary fighters when they traveled from Mexico to Cuba in 1956 to overthrow Fulgencio Batista's dictatorship. The name of the yacht comes from the English word "grandma".

Granma (newspaper): The name of the newspaper of record and official organ of the Central Committee of the Cuban Communist Party. It was named after the yacht "Granma".

Guagua: Bus.

Guajira, guajirita: Country girl.

Guanabacoa: One of the 15 municipalities in Havana, and a colonial township in the estearn part of the city.

Guarapo: Sugar cane juice.

Guerrillera: Woman guerrilla fighter.

Guerrillero Heroico: Heroic Guerrilla Fighter, referring to Ernesto *Che* Guevara.

Gusano, gusana: Worm, deserter.

Gusanería: Group of worms or deserters.

H

Habana Libre: One of the largest hotels in Cuba. It was opened in 1958 as "Habana Hilton" (a part of the American Hilton Hotels group), and then nationalized in 1960 and renamed *Habana Libre* (Free Havana).

Hembrera: A woman that conceives only girls. The word derives from *hembra*, female.

Hermana: Sister.

Hijo de puta: Son of a bitch.

Hojalatero: Man who collected tin.

Hola: Hello

I

Imperialismo yanqui: American imperialism.

Ingenio: Sugar cane factory.

Instituto: Institute, High School. It refers to the *Instituto de Segunda Enseñanza de La Habana*, Havana Secondary Education Institute.

Íntimas: Sanitary pads.

J

Jimagüas: Twins.

Jineteras: Female prostitutes whose clients are foreign tourists.

Joya: Perfume by Mirurgia, a Spanish Company.

Juventud Rebelde: Literally meaning "Rebel Youth". It is the newspaper of the Young Communist Union in Cuba (*Unión de Jóvenes Comunistas*).

K

Kotex: Refers to the American brand of feminine hygiene sanitary pads.

L

La Historia me absolverá: <u>History Will Absolve Me,</u> a speech made by Fidel Castro in his own defense in court, after attacking the Moncada Barracks in 1953. The speech was published later, and became the manifesto of the revolutionary movement against Fulgencio Batista's regime.

Libertad: Freedom.

Libreta (la libreta): Ration card.

Luz brillante: Kerosene

M

Machista: Sexist, male chauvinist.

Maja: Perfume by Mirurgia, a Spanish Company.

Malanga: The edible core of the tropical plant known as Taro or Eddoe, which is widely used in Cuba as baby food.

Malecón: The waterfront roadway and seawall of Havana which stretches for 8 km along the coast. It is a popular place for social gatherings.

Mandados: Shopping errands.

Maleconazo: The word derives from *Malecón*. The *Maleconazo* uprising was a protest against the Cuban government that took place on August 5th, 1994. Thousands of people spontaneously took the streets of Havana, starting at the *Malecón*, during the harshest phase of the Special Period (see

Período Especial). These protests, along with other events, prompted the "Rafter Crisis" (*Crisis de los balseros*), when more than 37,000 of Cubans left the island and headed to Florida, US, using self-constructed and very precarious vessels.

Mamá, mami: Mom.

Marcha del Pueblo Combatiente: March of the Fighting People.

Marginales: Marginals or delinquents.

Maricón: Pejorative word for homosexual, equivalent to the English *faggot*.

Mariel (El Mariel): It refers to the Mariel boatlift, a mass emigration of Cubans to the United States in 1980. The departure point of this exodus was the nearest Cuban port to the US: Mariel Harbor, located 25 miles west of Havana.

Mariposa: Butterfly.

Meprobamato: Meprobamate, a drug that works as an anxiolytic, used in Cuba mostly as a mild tranquilizer.

Mercados paralelos: Parallel markets, farmers markets.

Merienda: Snack.

Microbrigadas: Micro-brigades, construction work brigades created in the 70's to solve the housing problem in Cuba. Workers of any field could join a *microbrigada* to build apartments for themselves and other workers. Micro-brigades are infamous for the ugly designs and the bad quality of the buildings they constructed, as well as for the long construction delays due to lack of materials.

Mi'ja: My daughter, my girl. Contraction form of *mi hija*.

Miliciano/a: Member of the National Revolutionary Militia.

Militante: Member of the Communist Party.

Mima: Mom.

¡**Mi madre!**: Common expletive, literally meaning "Mother of mine!", roughly equivalent of "Oh, my God!"

MINCIN: Acronym for *Ministerio de Comercio Interior*, Ministry of Internal Commerce.

Moncadistas: The name given to children from 1st to 4th grade in primary school in Cuba, all of them compulsory members of the José Martí Pioneer Organization. The word derives from "Moncada", the name of the military barracks attacked by Fidel Castro and other revolutionary fighters in 1953.

Movimiento 26 de Julio: 26th of July Movement, the revolutionary organization Fidel Castro created in 1955 to overthrow Batista's regime in Cuba.

Mulata, mulatica: Mulatto woman, little mulatto girl.

N

Nailito: Small plastic bag.

Natillas de pan: Bread custard.

Nena: Girl

Negra, negro, el Negro:: Black woman, black man, the Black Man.

La Negra María: The black woman Maria.

El Negro: The black man.

Negrita: Black little girl.

Nevera: Cooler.

Niña (mi niña): Girl (my girl).

Norte (El Norte): North (The North), referring to the United States.

Ñ

Ñáñigo: Member of the *Abakuá* secret society (*Sociedad Secreta Abakuá*), an Afro-Cuban religious practice and male-only fraternity.

O

Ochún: *Orisha* or goddess of love, beauty, wealth and diplomacy in the Yoruba religion. In the Afro-Cuban *Santería* religion, *Ochún* is the goddess of rivers, love, femininity, beauty, maternity, and marriage. She is sometimes syncretistically identified with Our Lady of Charity (*la Virgen de la Caridad del Cobre*), Cuba's patron saint.

OFICODA: Acronym for *Oficina de Control y Distribución de Alimentos*, Office for Control of Food Distribution.

Once zapatos azul celeste: Literally meaning "Eleven light blue shoes." The phrase in Spanish contains a lot of "c" and "z," which in most of Spain are pronounced like /θ/ (similar to "**th**ing"), unlike the Latin American pronunciation that uses /s/ (similar to "**s**ack").

Opción Cero: Zero Option.

Oriente: Eastern part of the island.

Orishas: Spirits or deities in the Yoruba religious system.

P

Pachanga: Party, festive time.

Palacio de los deportes: Sport Arena.

Paladar: Small private restaurants, usually in private homes, run under strict supervision from the government.

Palero: Practitioners of the *Palo Monte Mayombe* religion, one of the most widespread religions of African descent in Cuba. *Monte* means "forest" and *palo* means "stick." The forest is the *paleros* church, and sticks of different plants are key elements in the practice of this Congo religion. *Paleros* are also referred as *mayomberos*, or male witches.

Papa: Potato.

Papá, pipo: Dad.

Paredón: Wall

Patio: Backyard.

¡Patria o Muerte! ¡Venceremos!: Homeland or Death! We will overcome!

Payama: Pajama.

Período Especial: Special Period, the economic crisis that began in Cuba in 1991, after the dissolution of the Soviet Union. Its full name was Special Period in Time of Peace.

Permuta: Exchange of one apartment or house for another.

Pesos: National Cuban currency.

Pesos convertibles: Convertible pesos. Exchangeable Cuban currency whose value is $1.00 USD, and $25.00 Cuban pesos. It only circulates within Cuba.

Picadillo de soya: Soy ground beef.

Pinchos: Slang word referring to the Cuban elite, people in high official positions or rank in the government.

Pingueros: Male prostitutes whose clients are foreign tourists.

Pioneros: Translates as "pioneers" and refers to all the youth groups related to the Communist Party of Cuba. Children become members of the *Pioneros* when they enter school. Although membership is voluntary, pressure is exerted to become a member of the organization.

Pitusa: Jeans.

Plátano: Plantain.

Plaza de la Revolución: Revolution Square.

Poder Popular: Literally meaning People's Power. It is short for *Asamblea Nacional del Poder Popular*, National Assembly of the People's Power, the legislative parliament of Cuba.

Polineuritis periférica: Peripheral neuropathy.

Presidente: President.

Prieto: Black man.

Prisión: Prison.

Puré San Germán: *San Germán* purée, one of the most popular and often the only availabe meal in the Cuba of the *Periodo Especial*. The purée was made of *chícharos* or yellow peas and water.

Q

Quilo: One cent.

Quince (Mis quince): Party for the fifteenth birthday celebration (My fifteen birthday party).

R

Radio Bemba: Word of mouth.

Radionovela: Radio play

Rendición de cuentas: See *Asamblea de Rendición de Cuentas*.

Revolución: Revolution

S

San Lázaro: Saint Lazarus

Santera: Female priest of the syncretistic Afro-Cuban religion known as *Santería* or *Regla de Ocha*. (For *Santería* see Note 16.)

Semi-internado: Half-day boarding school.

Señor: Mr.

Señora: Mrs. The lady of the house.

Señorita: Ms. Also, a girl becomes a *señorita* right after her first menstruation.

Sierra Maestra: Mountain range in the Cuban Eastern region of *Oriente*, where Fidel Castro and the guerrilla army were based, and from where they initiated the Revolution that overthrew the dictator Fulgencio Batista in 1959.

Sinvergüenza: Shameless.

¡Socialismo o muerte!: Socialism or Death!

Solar: Multiple dwelling units for poor families.

Solterona: Spinster.

Sopa de gallo: Literally meaning "rooster soup," but in Cuba it refers to water with brown sugar, a popular beverage during the `90s crisis.

Sorí Marín: Humberto Sorí Marín (1915-1961). After the revolutionary victory of 1959, he served as minister of agriculture but resigned shortly after, in May of the same year. After the Bay of Pigs Invasion, Sorí Marín was arrested and executed.

Sorpresa de pan: Bread surprise, meaning "another dish made with the bread."

T

Telenovela: Soap opera.

Tía: Aunt

Tortillera: Pejorative way to refer to lesbians.

U

UJC: Acronym for *Unión de Jóvenes Comunistas*, Young Communist Union. (See ***Juventud***)

UPC: Acronym for *Unión de Pioneros de Cuba*, Cuban Pioneers Union, created in 1962 and replaced by the "José Martí Pioneer Organization" (*Organización de Pioneros José Martí, OPJM*) in 1977.

V

Vale todo: Anything goes. It is the title of a very popular Brazilian soap opera which played on Cuban national TV during the `90s.

Venceremos: We will overcome.

Vieja, viejo: Literally, old woman or old man. In Cuba is also used as a form of addressing the mother, father, wife, husband or friends.

Viejo sinvergüenza: Shameless old man!

Vivienda: Short for *Instituto Nacional de la Vivienda*, National Institute of Housing.

Y

Yanquis: Americans.

Yuca: Manioc, yucca.

Yumas: Slang word for foreigners and tourists.

Z

Zafra: Sugar cane harvest.

About the Author

Dr. Araceli Alonso is a 2013 United Nations Award Winner for her public service and her activism on women's health and women right. She is currently an Associate Faculty at the University of Wisconsin-Madison in the Department of Gender and Women's Studies and in the School of Medicine and Public Health, where she teaches classes on women's health and women's rights. Alonso holds a Nursing degree, a Bachelors degree in History, a Master of Science, a Master of Arts, and a Ph.D. in Anthropology.

She is a professor, a writer, a women's rights activist, and a philanthropist. Doctor Alonso's multidisciplinary background has helped her work with women around the world in different circumstances, devoting the last twenty years to analyze women's health, women's rights, and women's empowerment cross-culturally. Alonso has extensive experience in conducting ethnographic research and fieldwork on women's lives in Spain, Cuba, Uganda, Kenya, and the United States. Her qualitative research skills became evident in the outcomes of her doctoral dissertation on Cuban women, which was awarded the Hyde Dissertation Research Award for Outstanding Dissertation Research in Gender and Women's Studies in 2002, and the Robert Miller Prize for Outstanding Dissertation Research in Anthropology in 2002.

Dr. Alonso is also the Founder and Director of the numerous award-winning non-profit organization called Health by Motorbike that provides a comprehensive model of health and well-being for women and children in rural communities of southeastern Kenya.

DEEP UNIVERSITY PRESS SCIENTIFIC BOARD MEMBERS

Dr. Ronald Arnett, Professor and chair, Communication & Rethoric Studies, Duquesne University, Pittsburgh, Pennsylvania

Dr. Gilles Baillat, Rector, ex-Director, Conference of Directors of Teacher Education University Institutes, University of Reims, France

Dr. Niels Brouwer, Graduate School of Education, Radboud Universiteit Nijmegen, The Netherlands

Dr. Yuangshan Chuang, President of APAMALL, NETPAW Director, Department of English, Kun Shan University, Taiwan, ROC

Dr. Enrique Correa Molina, Professor and Vice-Dean, Faculty of Education, University of Sherbrooke, Canada

Dr. José Correia, Dean, Faculty of Education, University of Porto, Portugal

Dr. Muhammet Demirbilek, Assistant Professor and Head, Educational Science Department, Suleyman Demirel University, Isparta, Turkey

Dr. Ángel Díaz-Barriga Casales, Professor, Autonomous National University of México UNAM (Mexico)

Dr. Bertha Du-Babcock, Professor, Department of English for Business, City University of Hong Kong, Hong Kong, China

Dr. Marc Durand, Professor, Faculty of Psychology and Education, University of Geneva, Switzerland

Dr. Paul Durning, Emeritus Professor, ex-Head of the Doctoral School, first Director of the French National Observatory, First vice president of EUSARF. University of Paris X Nanterre, France

Dr. Stephanie Fonvielle, Associate Professor, Teacher Education University Institute, University of Aix-Marseille, France

Dr. Mingle Gao, Dean, College of Education, Beijing Language and Culture University (BLCU), Beijing, China

Dr. Mercedes González Sanmamed, Professor at the University of A Coruña, Spain

Dr. Gabriela Hernández Vega, Professor at the University of Nariño, Colombia

Dr. Liliana Morandi, Associate Professor, National University of Rio

Cuarto, Cordoba, Argentina

Dr. Joëlle Morrissette, Professor, Department of Educational Psychology, Université of Montreal, Quebec, Canada

Dr. Martha Murzi Vivas, Professor, University of Los Andes, Venezuela

Dr. Thi Cuc Phuong Nguyen, Vice Rector, University of Hanoi, Hanoi, Vietnam

Dr. Shirley O'Neill, Associate Professor, President of the International Society for leadership in Pedagogies and Learning, University of Southern Queensland, Queensland Australia

Dr. José-Luis Ortega, Professor, Foreign Language Education, Faculty of Education, University of Granada, Spain

Dr. Surendra Pathak, Head and Professor, Department of Value Education, IASE University of Gandhi Viday Mandir, India

Dr. Luis Porta Vázquez, Professor at the National University of Mar del Plata CONICET (Argentina)

Dr. Shen Qi, Associate Professor, Shanghai Foreign Studies University (SHISU), Shanghai, China

Dr. Timothy Reagan, Professor and Dean of the Graduate School of Education, Nazarbayev University, Kazaksthan

Dr. Antonia Schleicher, Professor, NARLC Director and NCTOLCTL Executive Director, ACTFL Board member, Indiana University-Bloomington, USA

Dr. Farouk Y. Seif, Executive Director, Semiotic Society of America, Founding Director of Isis Institute, Professor Emeritus, Whole Systems Design, Center for Creative Change, Antioch University Seattle, Washington, USA

Dr. Gary Shank, Professor, Educational Foundations and Leadership, Duquesne University, Pittsburgh, Pennsylvania, USA

Dr. Kemal Silay, Professor and Director of the Flagship Program, Department of Central Eurasia, Indiana University-Bloomington, USA

Dr. José Tejada Fernández, Professor at the Autonomous University of Barcelona, Spain

Dr. Ronghui Zhao, Director, Institute of Linguistic Studies, Shanghai Foreign Studies University, Shanghai, China

Guide to Authors

What our Publishing Team can offer:

- An international editorial team, in more than 20 universities around the world.
- Dedicated and experienced topic editors who will review and provide feedback on your initial proposal.
- A specific format that will speed up the production of your book and its publication.
- Higher royalties than most publishers and a 20% discount on batch orders of 25+ copies.
- Global distribution and marketing through Amazon in the U.S., UK and other countries.
- Fast recognition of your work in your area of specialization.
- Quality design and affordable sales pricing. Using the latest technology, our books are produced efficiently, quickly and attractively.
- A global marketing plan, including electronic and web marketing and review mailing.
- Book Series: Deep Education; Deep Professional Development; Deep Language Learning; Signs & Symbols in Education; Language Education Policy; Deep Activism.

Deep University Online!

For updates and more resources
Visit the Deep University Website:

www.deepuniversity.com

publisher@deepuniversity.net

- ❖ The Author's Facebook group: https://www.facebook.com/araceli.alonso.549
- ❖ http://healthbymotorbike.wix.com/healthbymotorbike
- ❖ http://www.morgridge.wisc.edu/programs/awards/aracelialonso.html

Correspondence with the Author

Dr. Araceli Alonso, Department of Gender and Women Studies, School of Medicine and Public Health, UW-Madison, 3314 Sterling Hall, 475 N Charter St., Madison, Wisconsin 53706 USA.
E-mail: araalonso1@gmail.com

www.ingramcontent.com/pod-product-compliance
Lightning Source LLC
Chambersburg PA
CBHW030650230426
43665CB00011B/1037